Cambridge Certificate in Advanced English 5

WITH ANSWERS

Examination papers from University of Cambridge ESOL Examinations: English for Speakers of Other Languages

CAMBRIDGE
UNIVERSITY PRESS

CAMBRIDGE UNIVERSITY PRESS
Cambridge, New York, Melbourne, Madrid, Cape Town, Singapore, São Paulo

Cambridge University Press
The Edinburgh Building, Cambridge CB2 2RU, UK

www.cambridge.org
Information on this title: www.cambridge.org/9780521754378

First published 2003
4th printing 2005

Printed in the United Kingdom at the University Press, Cambridge

ISBN-13 978-0-521-75442-2 Student's Book
ISBN-10 0-521-75442-9 Student's Book

ISBN-13 978-0-521-75437-8 Student's Book with answers
ISBN-10 0-521-75437-2 Student's Book with answers

ISBN-13 978-0-521-75439-2 Teacher's Book
ISBN-10 0-521-75439-9 Teacher's Book

ISBN-13 978-0-521-75440-8 Set of 2 Cassettes
ISBN-10 0-521-75440-2 Set of 2 Cassettes

ISBN-13 978-0-521-75441-5 Set of 2 Audio CDs
ISBN-10 0-521-75441-0 Set of 2 Audio CDs

ISBN-13 978-0-521-75438-5 Self-study Pack
ISBN-10 0-521-75438-0 Self-study Pack

Contents

Acknowledgements   *iv*

To the student   *1*

Test 1   Paper 1   Reading   *4*
Paper 2   Writing   *13*
Paper 3   English in Use   *16*
Paper 4   Listening   *25*
Paper 5   Speaking   *29*

Test 2   Paper 1   Reading   *30*
Paper 2   Writing   *39*
Paper 3   English in Use   *42*
Paper 4   Listening   *51*
Paper 5   Speaking   *55*

Test 3   Paper 1   Reading   *56*
Paper 2   Writing   *65*
Paper 3   English in Use   *68*
Paper 4   Listening   *77*
Paper 5   Speaking   *81*

Test 4   Paper 1   Reading   *82*
Paper 2   Writing   *91*
Paper 3   English in Use   *94*
Paper 4   Listening   *103*
Paper 5   Speaking   *107*

Test 1   Key and transcript   *108*

Test 2   Key and transcript   *118*

Test 3   Key and transcript   *128*

Test 4   Key and transcript   *138*

Visual materials for Paper 5   *colour section*

Sample answer sheets   *148*

Acknowledgements

The publishers are grateful to the following for permission to reproduce copyright material. It has not always been possible to identify the sources of all the material used and in such cases the publishers would welcome information from the copyright owners.

The Times, 10 February 1994, for the article on pp. 6–7 by Richard Cork, 'The day I drew Picasso' © Times Newspapers Limited, London, and for the article on p. 44 from 'Case of jam today and jam yesterday', by Kevin Eason, *The Times*, 8 June 1996, and the extract on p. 57 'Is your office working' by Rachel Cooke, *The Times*, 8 January 1995; Anne Nicholls for the text on pp. 11–12, 'We changed lives for a day', published in *Living* September 1994, © Woman and Home/IPC Syndication; for the article 'Room at the Top' p. 25, copyright Halifax Building Society, Homes & Savings Magazine Autumn 1995; for the extract from *Careers in television and radio* by Michael Selby on p. 26, and for the text 'Being a theatre director' on p. 98, from *The Kogan Page Guide to Working in Arts, Craft and Design* by David Shacklady © Kogan Page 1997; Jonathan Burnham for paragraph C of the text, and Helen Fraser for paragraph A of the text 'Do reviews sell books?' on p. 31, published in the *Sunday Telegraph*, 1 January 1995; for the article on pp. 37–38, 'Take two careers' by Rebecca Cripps, © Marie Claire/IPC Syndication; Charles Clover for the article 'Solar survivor' on p. 60, first published in *Perspectives* October 1994; courtesy of *Cosmopolitan Magazine* © National Magazine Company for the article, 'Career Power' by Carole Pemberton on pp. 63–64 and for the article, 'Retreat, relax and re-charge', by Beverley D'Silva on p.83; *The Daily Telegraph*, 18 April 1996 for the article 'The Hotel Inspector' from 'A night with the avenging angel' by Christopher Middleton on p. 86; for the text 'Travelling through Norway' from *AA Great Railway Journeys of the World* on p. 96, reproduced by kind permission of the Automobile Association Developments Ltd LIC031/02.

For permission to reproduce copyright photographs:
Art Directors & TRIP/J King for p. C8 (centre left), /S Grant for p. C9 (bottom), /M Jelliffe for p. C10 (centre right), /D Saunders for p. C11 (top), /F Good for p. C11 (centre left), /R Vargas for p. C11 (centre right), /D Saunders for p. C13 (centre left), /F Good for p. C13 (centre right), /R Vargas for p. C11 (centre right), /E Young for p. C14 (bottom right), /E Young for p. C16 (centre); John Birdsall Photography for pp. C4 (top), C4 (centre), C4 (bottom), C5 (bottom), C10 (centre left); Collections/Roger Scruton for p. C2 (top), /George Wright for p. C7 (bottom); Corbis /Jose Juis Paelaez, Inc for p. C3 (centre left), /George Shelley, Inc for p. C3 (bottom left), /Owen Franken for p. C14 (top), /Owen Franken for p. C16 (bottom left); Getty Images for pp. C3 (top right), C3 (bottom right), C14 (bottom left), C15 (top right), C16 (top), /William R Sallaz for p. C2 (bottom right), /Jeff Cadge for p. C5 (top), /Dennie Cody for p. C6 (centre left), /Paul Souders for p. C6 (bottom right), /Paul Chesley for p. C8 (bottom left), /Hulton Archive, Fox Photos for p. C15 (bottom left); Sally & Richard Greenhill for p. C7 (top), /Richard Greenhill for p. C2 (bottom left), /Sally Greenhill for pp. C2 (centre right), C8 (top), and C8 (bottom right); Robert Harding Picture Library for p. C11 (bottom), p. C13 (top), /Roy Rainford for pp. C14 (centre) and C16 (bottom right), /Jean Brooks for p. C6 (top); Paul Mulcahy for p. C3 (top left); Pictures Colour Library for p C6 (centre right); Popperfoto for pp. C9 (top), C15 (centre left); Rex Features for p. C2 (centre left), /I.B.L. for p. C10 (bottom right); Royal Geographical Society, London/Hillary for p. C15 (centre right); Science Photo Library/Philippe Gontier/Eurelios for p. C10 (bottom left), /US Library of Congress for p. C15 (top left), /NASA for p. C15 (bottom right); Sporting Pictures (UK), for p. C10 (top); Tografox/Bob Battersby for p. C8 (centre right).

Picture research by Valerie Mulcahy

Design concept by Peter Ducker [MSTD]

Cover design by Dunne & Scully

The cassettes and audio CDs which accompany this book were recorded at Studio AVP, London

To *the student*

This book is for candidates preparing for the University of Cambridge ESOL Examinations Certificate in Advanced English (CAE). The CAE examination is widely recognised in commerce and industry and in individual university faculties and other educational institutions.

The collection of four complete practice tests comprises past papers from the Cambridge Certificate in Advanced English; you can practise these tests on your own or with the help of your teacher.

The CAE examination is part of a group of examinations developed by Cambridge ESOL called the Cambridge Main Suite. The Main Suite consists of five examinations which have similar characteristics but which are designed for different levels of English language ability. Within the five levels, CAE is at Cambridge/ALTE Level 4, Level C1 in the Council of Europe Framework and Level 2 in the UK National Qualifications Framework.

Examination	Cambridge/ALTE Level	Council of Europe Level	National Qualifications Framework Level
CPE Certificate of Proficiency in English	Level 5	C2	3
CAE Certificate in Advanced English	Level 4	C1	2
FCE First Certificate in English	Level 3	B2	1
PET Preliminary English Test	Level 2	B1	Entry 3
KET Key English Test	Level 1	A2	Entry 2
YLE Cambridge Young Learners English	Breakthrough Level		

The CAE examination consists of five papers:

Paper 1	**Reading**	1 hour 15 minutes
Paper 2	**Writing**	2 hours
Paper 3	**English in Use**	1 hour 30 minutes
Paper 4	**Listening**	45 minutes (approximately)
Paper 5	**Speaking**	15 minutes

Paper 1   Reading
This paper consists of four parts, each containing one text or several shorter pieces. The texts are taken from newspapers, magazines, non-literary books, leaflets, brochures, etc., and are selected to test a wide range of reading skills and strategies. There are between 40 and 50 multiple-matching, multiple-choice and gapped-text questions in total.

Paper 2   Writing
This paper consists of two parts and candidates have to complete two tasks (letters, reports, articles, competition entries, proposals, reviews and leaflets) of approximately 250 words each. **Part 1** consists of one compulsory task based on substantial reading input. **Part 2** consists of one task selected from a choice of four. Question 5 is always related to business. Assessment is based on content, organisation and cohesion, accuracy and range of language, register and effect on target reader.

Paper 3   English in Use
This paper consists of six parts designed to test the ability to apply knowledge of the language system, including vocabulary, grammar, spelling and punctuation, word-building, register and cohesion. It contains 80 items in total.

Part 1 is based on a short text and consists of a four-option multiple-choice cloze which focuses on vocabulary.

Part 2 is based on a short text and consists of a gap-fill exercise at word level which focuses on grammar.

Part 3 is based on a short text and is designed to test the ability to proofread and correct samples of written English. There are two types of task, either of which may be used in a test. In the first, candidates have to identify additional words which are incorporated in the text. In the second, candidates have to identify errors of spelling and punctuation.

Part 4 is based on two short texts and consists of a gap-fill exercise which focuses on word-building.

Part 5 is based on two short texts; the first text provides the input for the second text, which is a gap-fill exercise. This task focuses on the ability to re-write a given text in a different register.

Part 6 is based on a short text and consists of a gap-fill exercise at phrase or sentence level.

Paper 4   Listening
This paper consists of four parts each with texts of varying length and nature which test a wide range of listening skills. There are between 30 and 40 matching, completion and multiple-choice questions in total.

Paper 5   Speaking

Candidates are examined in pairs by two examiners, one taking the part of the Interlocutor and the other of the Assessor. The four parts of the test, which are based on visual stimuli and verbal prompts, are designed to elicit a wide range of speaking skills and strategies from both candidates.

Candidates are assessed individually. The Assessor focuses on grammar and vocabulary, discourse management, pronunciation, and interactive communication. The Interlocutor provides a global mark for the whole test.

Marks and results

Each paper is weighted to 40 marks. Therefore, the five CAE papers total 200 marks, after weighting.

Your overall CAE grade is based on the total score gained in all five papers. It is not necessary to achieve a satisfactory level in all five papers in order to pass the examination with grade A, B or C. A is the highest. The minimum successful performance in order to achieve grade C corresponds to about 60% of the total marks. D and E are failing grades.

Your Statement of Results will include a graphical profile of your performance in each paper and show your relative performance in each one.

The CAE examination is recognised by the majority of British universities for English language entrance requirements.

Further information

For more information about CAE or any other Cambridge ESOL examination write to:

EFL Division
University of Cambridge ESOL Examinations
1 Hills Road
Cambridge
CB1 2EU
England

Tel: +44 1223 553997
Fax: +44 1223 460278
e-mail: efl@ucles.org.uk
http://www.CambridgeESOL.org

In some areas, this information can also be obtained from the British Council.

Test 1

PAPER 1   READING (1 hour 15 minutes)

Part 1

Answer questions **1–14** by referring to the book reviews on page **5**. Indicate your answers **on the separate answer sheet**.

For questions **1–14**, match each of the statements below with one of the books (**A–E**) reviewed on page **5**. Some of the choices may be required more than once.

Which book

describes the results of one person's uncharacteristic behaviour?	**1** ....
has a main character who is reluctant to accept a diminishing role?	**2** ....
is considered a challenging read?	**3** ....
reveals the unhappiness hidden in people's lives?	**4** ....
looks at the relationships between two people from different backgrounds?	**5** ...B.....
explores the unchanging nature of life in the country?	**6** ....
is praised for its originality?	**7** ...A.....
deals with the characters' attempts to reach a deeper understanding of themselves?	**8** ....
focuses on a character who is both appealing and scheming?	**9** ....
conveys a character's feelings of inadequacy?	**10** ....
features a main character whose views on traditional ways of life undergo a change?	**11** ....
deals with the activities of someone living in an invented world?	**12** ...A.....
is written in a similar style to a previous novel?	**13** ....
focuses on how people cope with disruption in their lives?	**14** ...B.....

New In Paperback

A

The career of citizen Tristan Smith, set in the fictional republic of Efica, is an extraordinary parable of human power, history and humour. In a feat of considerable literary skill, the author has created a world with its own history, traditions and customs.

The book is notable also for its humour, and for the author's unique vision, which is here combined with his penetrating psychological insight in a novel which is difficult but rewarding.

B

Harriet is poised and middle-class, with an architect husband and her own business. Ordinarily, she would never have met Sheila, a traditional working-class woman who looks after her ageing father and has brought up her grandson, Leo, since he was three.

Their lives are shattered when the teenage Leo viciously attacks Harriet's son, Joe, in the street. After the court case both boys refuse to talk about what happened. Leo, who had been a model pupil and had never been involved in a fight before, will not explain what came over him, while Joe recovers physically but becomes withdrawn. Harriet is tortured by the effect on her son and ministering to him takes over her life. Sheila is so wracked with guilt that she requests a meeting – from which their unusual friendship grows.

The great strength of the author has always been in depicting how people react to upheaval in their lives. He also captures the mother's sense that, no matter how hard she tries, she can never do enough.

C

Shortlisted for the Booker prize, this book follows the fortunes of one of the most isolated of the Scottish Orkney islands and its inhabitants over a long and uneventful rural history.

The book sets this narrative against pertinent moments in Scottish history, as vividly imagined in the daydreams of the young protagonist, Throfinn Ragnarson, who disappears abruptly at one point in the book, only to return after the Second World War, having now learnt to appreciate the simplicity of his worthy ancestors' lives.

D

Following his recent blockbuster success, the author has produced a sequel resonant with the same gentle irony and acid observations of family life which made its predecessor so appealing.

Fifteen years after her daughter's death, Aurora Greenway approaches her seventies with her spirited companion, Rosie Sunlap. Aurora's approach to life remains the same winning combination of vanity, charm and reluctant kindness, and Rosie provides an ally in her continuing and highly enjoyable manipulation of both suitors and friends. By the end of the book, Aurora is forced to acknowledge the passage of time that brings a new generation to centre stage.

The author is skilful at exposing the haunting sadness that hovers beneath the seeming ordinariness of life. He is attuned more to the shadows than the bright lights of human activity and identifies the randomness of events.

E

Six disparate people are brought together by millionaire Logan Urquhart to sail around the islands of the South Pacific in his yacht, the *Ardent Spirit*. With her awe-inspiring mastery of descriptive language, the author charts the personal voyages of self-discovery with which each of these mariners prepares to return home, their own spirits quickened and made ardent by the experience of life adrift on 'the desert cities of waves'.

The author uses startling images to convey her themes of memory and awareness. Those images are both alienating and illuminating.

Part 2

For questions **15–21**, you must choose which of the paragraphs **A–H** on page **7** fit into the numbered gaps in the following newspaper article. There is one extra paragraph which does not fit in any of the gaps. Indicate your answers **on the separate answer sheet**.

The day I drew Picasso

Richard Cork recalls how, as an 18-year-old student, he came face-to-face with one of the most revered artists of the century.

Even seen at a distance, eating his lunch at an open-air restaurant in Cannes harbour, Picasso was instantly recognisable. I was an 18-year-old student, filling in time before university by travelling round Europe and Morocco in a battered and unreliable van. Having run out of money, I found a boat-painting job on the waterfront. But I spent much of the time drawing, and was lucky enough to be carrying an ample sketchbook when my encounter with the octogenarian artist took place.

15

But my request was generously granted. Taking the large sheet I passed over, Picasso inscribed his name across the top of the paper. Then, as if unable to resist the blankness below, he added an exuberant linear flourish on the rest of the page. But Picasso's art, even at its least representational, was usually anchored in observed reality. So the curves may well refer to a cloud, the wind-rippled sea or the shape assumed by Cannes harbour, dominating his lunchtime vantage point.

16

After a while, I returned to the boat and proudly displayed the fruit of my visit. But the friend who had encouraged me to introduce myself to Picasso could see that the lunch party was still in progress. 'Is that all?' he asked, looking at the signature. 'Why on earth don't you go back and make the most of it? You won't get a chance like this again – and he probably wouldn't mind if you drew his portrait.'

17

Once he noticed, Picasso grinned like an imp and made my task wickedly difficult. He acted out a range of expressions, both ridiculous and macabre – rolling his eyes, sticking out his tongue and brandishing his hand in fantastical shapes on either side of his forehead. The entire performance was carried out with the gusto of an instinctive clown.

18

As if to bear this out, Picasso at last relented and lapsed into repose. For a few extraordinary minutes, he deliberately gave me the chance to study him without impediment. I noticed how tough and alert he appeared, still taut in a blue-and-white striped jersey. As compact as a wrestler, the deeply tanned figure resembled an athletic 60-year-old rather than a man who would soon be celebrating his 84th birthday.

19

He also seemed curiously removed and alone, even though there was plenty of company nearby. His engaging burst of buffoonery could not disguise an underlying gravity of spirit. Content to let his friends do most of the talking, he sat in a very private and absorbed silence, pursuing his own isolated interests undisturbed.

When the American lady told me that 'the Maestro' wanted to see his portrait, I became embarrassed and replied that it wasn't good enough to show him. Picasso insisted, however, and after I passed my sketchbook over, he gave my efforts a generous nod.

20

He handed the pad back, and there was a drawing blithely at odds with my dogged strivings. Picasso had moved one eye onto my nose, and summarised my smile in a single, irresistibly vivacious line. I looked like a creature who had strayed from one of his more lighthearted mythological compositions. Perhaps he saw me

as an intruder from another world, peering in at him with all the gauche curiosity of a young man amazed to find himself face-to-face with an artist he venerated.

21

All the same, I look back now and wonder at my good fortune. Meeting Picasso and, more important, receiving his attention meant an enormous amount to me.

A Sketchbook under arm, I returned to Picasso's table. I thought it wise not to ask him whether he'd mind having his portrait drawn: a refusal at this stage might have wrecked the whole delicate enterprise. So I simply stood by the table, propped my pad against an ironwork screen, got out a stick of crayon and started to draw.

B Today, when I view the sheet with the two portraits, I am impressed above all by the salutary contrast between my tentative draughtsmanship and the joyful, effortless virtuosity of the face summarised beneath.

C Picasso was known to be a fairly reclusive figure who spent most of his time shut away working high in the hills. So I was doubly astonished to find him seated at a table with his wife, Jacqueline, and three companions. Without my friend's prompting, I would never have dared to walk over and ask for his signature. Nor did I imagine, as I nervously introduced myself and offered my sketchbook, that he would comply.

D I marvelled at the youthfulness of his clear, dark eyes, set with startling intensity in features remarkably unencumbered by the folds of slack flesh on so many elderly faces. The eyes were mesmerising, and I tried to give them the necessary forcefulness. After fastening themselves on whatever they wanted to scrutinise, they did not blink until the unwavering gaze moved elsewhere.

E I was tempted to give up the struggle, but the sheer high spirits of my playful sitter seemed tantamount to a challenge. However obstructive his antics, I felt that he was testing my persistence, in order, perhaps, to discover the true extent of my determination.

F I thanked Picasso, and asked him if he would be kind enough to sign the drawing. After consultation, the American explained that 'the Maestro says you already have his signature'. So there were limits to the generosity he was prepared to bestow on me!

G Then, to my astonishment, he announced that it was now his turn. I lost no time in giving him my crayon, and his hand applied a few swift, decisive strokes to the paper. In a matter of seconds, with beguiling assurance, he outlined a bearded face below the head which had taken me so many anxious minutes to produce.

H Delighted, I thanked him and embarked on a halting conversation. Since Picasso's English was even poorer than my French, an extravagantly dressed American woman at the table acted as our interpreter. She kept describing him as 'the Maestro', and it was difficult to combat her gushing interjections. But I did manage to tell Picasso of my voracious interest in art and my admiration for his work.

Part 3

Read the following magazine article and answer questions **22–28** on page **9**. **On your answer sheet**, indicate the letter **A**, **B**, **C** or **D** against the number of each question. Give only one answer to each question.

P.D. James

Barbara Michaels meets the acclaimed crime writer, whose innocent exterior hides a complex and brilliant imagination.

Best-selling crime writer P.D. James – the initials stand for Phyllis Dorothy – exudes an air of quiet authority. It is easy to envisage her, had she not become a creator of detective stories with more twists and turns than a spiral staircase, as a headmistress of a girls' school. But it is soon apparent from what she says that the authoritative mien is, in fact, a cloak for shyness. She reluctantly admits that Adam Dalgliesh, the detective in her novels, 'is, I suppose, modelled on myself – or rather, the way I would have turned out if I had been a man'. Dalgliesh prefers to unravel the complexities of crimes solo, as does his creator. 'I need time on my own, particularly when I am writing. I can write more or less anywhere as long as I have total privacy.'

She is too modest to concur with the view that she is Britain's best-known crime writer, even though her books – 12 major detective novels – are read avidly by millions all over the world. She herself is a great fan of the works of close friend Ruth Rendell. 'I particularly enjoy her psychological works, written under the name of Barbara Vine.' Books beside her bed are most likely to be by women writers such as Iris Murdoch, Anita Brookner and Penelope Lively, although not to the total exclusion of male authors like Graham Greene and Evelyn Waugh, whom she considers to have been the greatest novelists of their generation.

Success came to P.D. James late in life. Now in her seventies, she was 42 when her first crime novel, *Cover Her Face*, was published. Born in Oxford, the eldest of three children, Phyllis grew up mainly in Cambridge, where her family moved when she was 11 years old. 'I met my husband there – he was a student at the university, and I have always loved the place. That is why I chose it as the setting for *An Unsuitable Job For A Woman.*'

Reluctantly, she reveals that from a promising start, life has been hard, even tragic at times. Her Irish doctor husband, Connor Bantry White,

returned from the Second World War, during which he served with the Royal Army Medical Corps, a very sick man. 'I had to work long hours to support him and our two young daughters, Clare and Jane. The ideas were teeming in my head, but I could do practically nothing about it – I simply hadn't the time. My husband's parents, however, were marvellous, and took my daughters under their wing, giving them a sense of security throughout those difficult years.'

While working full-time in administration for the National Health Service, she made good use of her enviable organisational skills. At one point, five psychiatric outpatients' clinics came under her jurisdiction. Then followed 11 years at the Home Office, first in the Police Department, doing administration for forensic science research, and then in the Criminal Law section, in the juvenile crime division. It was while working in forensic science that she became 'quite accustomed' to the sight of corpses. But it was not fascination with death itself that inspired her. 'It was, rather, the shape and construction involved in the writing of a crime novel that appealed. I have always enjoyed reading detective stories, and I always knew that I wanted to be a writer.'

'I didn't want to use the traumatic events of my own life in a work of fiction. The writing of a detective story appealed as a wonderful apprenticeship for someone setting out to be a serious novelist, and it was suitably removed from my own experience. As I went on, I became increasingly aware that one could stay within the constraints and indeed within the so-called formula of the classic detective story and still write a good, serious and revealing novel about human beings. Writing detective stories', she says, 'is a way of bringing order out of disorder. The solution of a crime confirms the sanctity of life – even if that life is unlovable. Nobody really likes violence.'

22 What does the writer suggest about P.D. James's outward manner?

    A It is an attempt to discourage curiosity.
    B It points to a lack of self-confidence.
    C It conceals the true nature of her personality.
    D It comes as a surprise to her readers.

23 When questioned about Adam Dalgliesh, P.D. James

    A concedes that the detective resembles her.
    B admits that his behaviour is unusual.
    C accepts that he does not enjoy company.
    D recognises a weakness in the detective's character.

24 What is revealed about P.D. James's tastes in reading?

    A She prefers books with lots of action.
    B She is less keen on male than female writers.
    C She believes that men write better books than women.
    D She thinks that women writers are not given enough credit.

25 According to P.D. James, her early writing career suffered from lack of

    A support.
    B commitment.
    C confidence.
    D opportunity.

26 What characterised P.D. James's work in the National Health Service?

    A It was well-suited to her talents.
    B It was not a satisfying experience.
    C It was useful for her future writing.
    D It was not sufficiently demanding.

27 P.D. James was drawn to writing crime novels because

    A they were her favourite sort of reading.
    B they would be useful to her in her career.
    C she liked the technical challenge they offered.
    D she had experienced the effects of crime at first hand.

28 What realisation did P.D. James come to while working on her detective stories?

    A It was not necessary to pay attention to established patterns.
    B The conventions did not adversely affect the quality of her writing.
    C It was inevitable that she would become emotionally involved.
    D The subject matter was more limiting than she had expected.

Part 4

Answer questions **29–47** by referring to the magazine article on pages **11–12** about people exchanging occupations. Indicate your answers **on the separate answer sheet**.

For questions **29–47**, answer by choosing from the people (**A–D**) on the right below. Some of the choices may be required more than once.

Which of the people A–D states the following about her day?

She wasn't sure what clothes would be appropriate.	**29** ....
She particularly enjoyed a quiet period during the day.	**30** ....
She was surprised by a comment someone made.	**31** ....
She felt the lack of companionship.	**32** ....
She didn't want to appear out of place.	**33** ....
She had misjudged the type of personality required for the job.	**34** ....
She had been made aware beforehand of a possible problem.	**35** ....
She had difficulty mastering one of the required skills.	**36** ....
She found it hard to resist a temptation.	**37** ....
She felt that remaining calm would be the best tactic at one point.	**38** ....

A   Amanda

B   Cindy

Which of the people A–D refers to

C   Rosemary

an advantage of the other person's occupation?	**39** ....
the realisation that attempts were being made to trick her?	**40** ....
a concern that proved unnecessary because of equipment provided?	**41** ....
being out of practice at something?	**42** ....
her certainty that she would be able to cope?	**43** ....
agreeing to get involved in an activity?	**44** ....
a working method that had changed since she was young?	**45** ....
a phrase that she implies could be more simply expressed?	**46** ....
her failure to impress other people?	**47** ....

D   Hilary

We changed lives for a day!

Have you ever dreamed about swapping lives with someone else for a day? Perhaps you think it would be more fun to do something quite different for a change? We fixed it for four people – read how it went.

Amanda (23), a young mother with two daughters, swapped lives with her friend Cindy (30), who works as a waitress at a glitzy London restaurant and entertainment complex.

A Amanda's story

I'd never been inside anywhere remotely like it before. I couldn't believe how dark and noisy it was – there were so many people and such a brilliant atmosphere. It was all a far cry from my home town and, to be honest, I wasn't sure I'd survive! Being a mother is definitely a busy job – but this was something else!

I had just fifteen minutes to learn how to carry a tray of drinks at shoulder height with one hand. The other waitresses made it look so simple, but just as I was getting the hang of it, the drinks started to slide off the tray and crashed on to the floor, splattering cocktails everywhere. I was so embarrassed, but all the other waitresses laughed. Everyone makes a fool of themselves at first!

By opening time at 11.30 am, a queue had already formed outside and I began to feel really nervous. I was worried about how I'd remember all the orders, but that, at least, wasn't a problem because everything was automated.

After a couple of hours my feet really ached and I couldn't get used to the constant loud music. Every time a customer spoke to me I had to say 'Pardon?', which was so embarrassing! By the end of my shift at 5 pm, I was totally exhausted and longed to soak my feet in a bowl of hot water. I couldn't believe it when one of the waitresses told me it had been a 'quiet' day!

I never realised how tiring waitressing would be. I've always thought it was a job for shrinking violets, but in fact you definitely need to be quite bubbly, as well as having the ability to keep a cool head and deal with what is known in the trade as a 'high-volume experience' – in other words, lots of customers!

I'm really quite shy and I don't think I could cope on a Saturday night, when it gets chaotically busy. I wasn't too impressed with the pay either. Unfortunately, I must have been a lousy waitress because even the rich Americans didn't tip me a bean!

I must admit I was very glad to get back to my children. It seems quite easy after waitressing!

B Cindy's story

I was feeling quite apprehensive about being a 'mum' for the day, but I was looking forward to it, too. I'd been warned the girls were cheeky, but in my ignorance I thought I could handle it. Little did I know!

As Amanda left to make her way to the restaurant, I had to get the two girls dressed and fed. After dropping off Sophie at school and Katie at nursery I thought I'd have three hours of peace. Wrong! A note from Amanda reminded me that I still had to make the beds, clean the house and do the washing.

At 1 pm I picked up Katie, whizzed around the supermarket and then took her home for lunch. But it was when I brought Sophie home from school that the real trouble started. They turned the settee into a trampoline and played a game which involved screaming as loudly as they possibly could! I decided to take the laid-back approach, imagining they'd soon get worn out. Wrong again. I thought I had a fair amount of stamina, but they beat me, hands down!

After much persuasion, I managed to get them into bed by about 8 pm, but then the fun and games started! How many glasses of water can a child drink, for heaven's sake? Of course, I realised it was just a ploy so they could come downstairs and watch television, but it was exhausting to spend all evening negotiating deals with them.

I never realised how tiring it could be looking after two small children. You don't get a second to think about yourself – and the sheer sense of responsibility is overwhelming. Even so, I really enjoyed the day.

Rosemary (42) runs a dairy farm. She swapped with Hilary (30), a teacher at a primary school.

C   Rosemary's story

On the farm, I have to get up at 5.30 am so sleeping in until 7 was pure luxury! But I dithered for ages about how to look. I could hardly turn up in overalls and boots, could I?

Looking at a sea of faces – about 400 pupils – at assembly, I hoped I melted into the background and that my fresh complexion didn't make me stand out as being straight off the farm.

After that it was time for a maths class. The children worked in small groups, using workcards graded according to difficulty – rather different from when I was at school and we had to recite tables in unison! Then I helped out with a nature project – identifying and feeding species of snails.

By lunchtime I was exhausted and looking forward to an hour's break, but the teachers only have about five minutes to eat their meal. There's so much to do before classes start again. I attended a staff meeting about reports and couldn't avoid getting roped in to help with athletics trials.

After lunch there was a silent reading lesson (bliss!) and then a French lesson in the video room. This was great fun because all the children wanted to practise on me, which really showed up my rusty French.

Finally we moved on to the school hall for Physical Education. I was drained by now, but the children seemed to have inexhaustible energy.

The hardest part of the job was standing up in front of the class and speaking – even for just two minutes, it's daunting. Teachers may get more holidays a year, but I think I'll stick to farming, anyway!

D   Hilary's story

I arrived at White House Farm at 8.30 am, bright and early, only to discover that Rosemary had been up for three hours! Rosemary's 280-acre farm has 100 Jersey cows, 15 calves and heifers and about 800 ewes! As well as milk, she manufactures ice-cream, yoghurt and cream, which is sold in shops, restaurants and at tourist attractions. I spent most of the morning in the ice-cream parlour, bottling milk into plastic litre containers, squeezing ice-cream from a machine into cartons and sticking on labels. It was difficult to stop myself dipping my fingers into the goodies! At lunchtime it was time to inspect the sheep. I drove over to one of the fields and picked up a ewe which had fallen over. If the sheep are left for more than 12 hours once they have fallen over they could die, so they have to be checked every day. What a nightmare it must be in winter!

After feeding the calves, I started the milking. The process took an exhausting two-and-a-half hours. And Rosemary does this twice a day, starting at 6 am, seven days a week, 365 days a year!

I found it quite a lonely day. I was surprised how much I missed the children – animals don't answer back! The worst aspect of the job is not being able to get away from work. The cows always have to be milked twice a day, so it's really difficult to plan any time off. Rosemary will only get about three days' holiday this year.

Farming seems romantic but the reality is very different. The income is irregular and I'd hate to be at the mercy of the weather.

PAPER 2   WRITING (2 hours)

Part 1

1 You are studying at a college called the Language Institute. Following serious complaints from students, your college Principal has agreed to improve the food and service offered in the college canteen. Proposals have been invited from catering companies. The Principal has shortlisted three, and has asked you, as a member of the student social committee, to advise on an appropriate choice.

Read the article below about the students' complaints and the three proposals which follow. Then, **using the information appropriately**, write a report for the Principal in which you assess the advantages and disadvantages of **all three** proposals and recommend **one**, justifying your choice.

**STUDENTS'
PROTEST**

Students are refusing to use the canteen at the Language Institute. A demonstration was held at the main entrance yesterday.

The students are complaining of:
• unhealthy food
• little choice
• high prices
• unfriendly staff
• limited opening hours.

Kavanagh Catering Services

Proposal for Language Institute Canteen

Introduction
Our aim is to give you good food at low cost. We believe in fast but friendly service, and value for money.

Food and Drink
We offer basic food at basic prices. Fast food, snacks and some hot meals would be available throughout the day and early evening. Sample menus on request.

Opening hours
From breakfast at 8 am to 8 pm.

Rainbow Ltd

Proposal for Language Institute Canteen

We aim to provide a variety of healthy food in a relaxing atmosphere.

The food
We offer a wide choice of hot dishes each day, including a vegetarian option, plus a selection of salads. There would always be a good range of snack food available. Our meals are always made from fresh ingredients.

Opening hours
Open from 9 am until 6 pm, with drinks and snacks constantly available (hot meals 12–2 only).

Xanadu Express

Proposal: Language Institute Canteen

Xanadu offers top-quality, world-wide cuisine, nutritious food and a friendly welcome.

Menu changes daily. A choice of two hot dishes each day. Full meals always available. Wide range of drinks including herbal teas and good coffee.

Opening hours: 8 am to 10 pm

Now write your **report** for the college Principal (approximately 250 words). You should use your own words as far as possible.

Part 2

Choose **one** of the following writing tasks. Your answer should follow exactly the instructions given. Write approximately 250 words.

2   You see the announcement below in *Modern World*, an international magazine.

> ### NEW TECHNOLOGY AND YOU
>
> We invite you, our readers, to submit an article on new technology and how it affects your life. We will publish one article from each country.
>
> Your article should outline the impact of new technology on your life now. You should also explain what further changes are likely to take place in the near future and how these could affect you.

Write your **article**.

3   You see this competition in an English language magazine.

> **If you really want to learn English you should get a job in an English-speaking country, speak to the people and travel around.**

Do you agree with this opinion? Give us your reasons why or why not. The best answer will win a ticket to London.

Write your **competition entry**, giving your views.

4   You see the following announcement in an in-flight magazine.

> ### A MEMORABLE EVENT
>
> Have you recently attended a special event of local or national importance which was particularly memorable for you? We would like to know why this event took place, what happened, and most importantly, the effect it had on you.
>
> The most interesting account will be published in next month's magazine.

Write your **account**.

5   An international business magazine has asked readers to name a book which has helped them in their job. Write a review for the magazine including:
   • the name of the book
   • a brief summary of the contents
   • what you personally learned from the book
   • how it may help other people in their work.

Write your **review**.

PAPER 3   ENGLISH IN USE (1 hour 30 minutes)

Part 1

For questions **1–15**, read the article below and then decide which word on page **17** best fits each space. Put the letter you choose for each question in the correct box on your answer sheet. The exercise begins with an example (**0**).

Example:

0	*B*	0

SECRETARIES

What's in a name? In the case of the secretary, it can be something rather surprising. The dictionary calls a secretary 'anyone who **(0)** ..... correspondence, keeps records and does clerical work for others'. But while this particular job **(1)** ..... looks a bit **(2)** ....., the word's original meaning is a hundred times more exotic and perhaps more **(3)** ..... . The word itself has been with us since the 14th century and comes from the mediaeval Latin word *secretarius* meaning 'something hidden'. Secretaries started out as those members of staff with knowledge hidden from others, the silent ones mysteriously **(4)** ..... the secret machinery of organisations.

A few years ago 'something hidden' probably meant **(5)** ..... out of sight, tucked away with all the other secretaries and typists. A good secretary was an unremarkable one, efficiently **(6)** ..... orders, and then returning mouse-like to his or her station behind the typewriter, but, with the **(7)** ..... of new technology, the job **(8)** ..... upgraded itself and the role has changed to one closer to the original meaning. The skills required are more **(9)** ..... and more technical. Companies are **(10)** ..... that secretarial staff should already be **(11)** ..... trained in, or at least familiar with, a **(12)** ..... of word processing packages. In addition to this they need the management skills to take on some administration, some personnel work and some research. The professionals in the **(13)** ..... business see all these developments as **(14)** ..... the jobs which secretaries are being asked to do.

It may also encourage a dramatic **(15)** ..... in office practice. In the past it was usual to regard the secretary as almost dehumanised, to be seen and not heard.

0 **A** orders (**B**) handles **C** runs **D** controls

1 **A** explanation **B** detail **C** definition **D** characteristic

2 **A** elderly **B** unfashionable **C** outdated **D** aged

3 **A** characteristic **B** related **C** likely **D** appropriate

4 **A** operating **B** pushing **C** vibrating **D** effecting

5 **A** kept **B** covered **C** packed **D** held

6 **A** satisfying **B** obeying **C** completing **D** minding

7 **A** advent **B** approach **C** entrance **D** opening

8 **A** truly **B** validly **C** correctly **D** effectively

9 **A** thorough **B** demanding **C** severe **D** critical

10 **A** insisting **B** ordering **C** claiming **D** pressing

11 **A** considerably **B** highly **C** vastly **D** supremely

12 **A** group **B** collection **C** cluster **D** range

13 **A** appointment **B** hiring **C** recruitment **D** engagement

14 **A** improving **B** intensifying **C** advancing **D** heightening

15 **A** turn **B** change **C** switch **D** swing

Part 2

For questions **16–30**, complete the following article by writing each missing word in the correct box on your answer sheet. **Use only one word for each space.** The exercise begins with an example (**0**).

Example:

0	*its*	0
		_ _

The Legend of the Root

Ginseng is one of the great mysteries of the east. Often referred to as the 'elixir of life', **(0)** ..... widespread use in oriental medicine has led **(16)** ..... many myths and legends building up around this remarkable plant. Ginseng has featured **(17)** ..... an active ingredient in oriental medical literature for over 5,000 years. Its beneficial effects were, at one time, **(18)** ..... widely recognised and praised that the root was said to **(19)** ..... worth its weight in gold.

(20) ..... the long history of ginseng, no one fully knows how it works. The active part of the plant is the root. Its full name is Panax Ginseng – the word Panax, **(21)** ..... the word panacea, coming from the Greek for 'all healing'. There is growing interest by western scientists **(22)** ..... the study of ginseng. It is today believed that **(23)** ..... remarkable plant may **(24)** ..... beneficial effects in the treatment of many diseases **(25)** ..... are difficult to treat with synthetic drugs.

Today, ginseng is **(26)** ..... longer a myth or a legend. Throughout the world **(27)** ..... is becoming widely recognised that this ancient herb holds the answer to relieving the stresses and ailments of modern living. It is widely used for the treatment of various ailments **(28)** ..... as arthritis, diabetes, insomnia, hepatitis and anaemia. However, the truth behind **(29)** ..... ginseng works still remains a mystery. Yet its widespread effectiveness shows that the remarkable properties are **(30)** ..... than just a legend.

Part 3

In **most** lines of the following text, there is **either** a spelling **or** a punctuation error. For each numbered line **31–46**, write the correctly spelt word or show the correct punctuation in the box on your answer sheet. **Some lines are correct.** Indicate these lines with a tick (✓) in the box. The exercise begins with three examples (**0**), (**00**) and (**000**).

Examples:

0	*speech?*	0
00	*attempts*	00
000	✔	000

Artificial Speech

0	Is it possible to construct devices that will talk and understand speech
00	As early as the 18th century, various atempts were being made to find
000	some way of reproducing the human voice by mechanical means. The
31	austrian inventor, Wolfgang von Kempelen (1734–1804) built a small
32	maschine consisting of a device to produce air flow, and other similar
33	mechanisms to function like a voice box Alexander Bell (1847–1922)
34	also constructed a 'talking head', made out of artificial materials which
35	was able to produce a few sounds. Modern techniques have lead to
36	huge progress in this field. It is no longer neccessary to build physical
37	models of the voice box as sound waves can be made electronicly by
38	reproducing the different components of the sound wave. Early results
39	sounded very unnatural. More recently the quality of artificial speech
40	has greatly improved. In fact, with some devices, it is impossible to tell
41	whether or not a human being is talking. In most cases, however there
42	are still problems of clarity and naturalness to be overcome, especially
43	those of rhythm and intonation. Present automatic talker's are limited
44	in what they are able to say. But currant work in artificial intelligence
45	means that speech can be produced from a devices own 'knowledge'.
46	This exciting development is considered to be an important area of
	present-day research.

Part 4

For questions **47–61**, read the two texts on pages **20** and **21**. Use the words in the boxes to the right of the texts to form **one** word that fits in the same numbered space in the text. Write the new word in the correct box on your answer sheet. The exercise begins with an example (**0**).

Example:

0	*classical*	0

ADVERTISEMENT FOR UNIVERSITY COURSES

Music Department
New Courses

Mozart's Chamber Music   Tuesdays 7.30 pm – 9.30 pm

Mozart's chamber works represent the summit of (**0**) ..... attainment. Students will be introduced to several of his finest (**47**) ..... , with particular (**48**) ..... on examining a variety of instrumental forms: string quartet, trio, sonata, quintet, etc. No (**49**) ..... musical expertise is required, although student (**50**) ..... during discussion of the works will be encouraged.

Music and Literature   Wednesdays 10 am – 12 noon

Music and literature generate great emotion, but they appear to work in different ways. This course examines the (**51**) ..... between these art forms and their (**52**) ..... of similar themes. Course materials will come from a wide range of both musical and (**53**) ..... genres, including sound, opera and oratoria, poetry, the novel and drama.

(**0**)	**CLASSIC**
(**47**)	COMPOSE
(**48**)	EMPHASISE
(**49**)	PRACTICE
(**50**)	PUT
(**51**)	CONNECT
(**52**)	TREAT
(**53**)	LITERATE

EXTRACT FROM A MAGAZINE ARTICLE

Home from Home

Media attention has **(54)** ..... the appeal of home exchange over the past few years and many thousands of people make **(55)** ..... to exchange their homes in order to provide a holiday either in the UK or **(56)** ..... .

Awareness of such schemes has grown **(57)** ..... , particularly in North America, which has increased the choice of exchange homes available. This can be a neat holiday **(58)** ..... for those who prefer more freedom and **(59)** ..... when on holiday. However, it is only really suitable for those who have few anxieties about their own homes being occupied in their **(60)** ..... .

Aside from the obvious cost advantage, there is the **(61)** ..... of self-catering and the opportunity to see beyond the normal tourist experience.

(54)	WIDE
(55)	ARRANGE
(56)	SEA
(57)	DRAMA
(58)	SOLVE
(59)	DEPEND
(60)	ABSENT
(61)	FLEXIBLE

Part 5

For questions **62–74**, read the following memorandum and use the information in it to complete the numbered gaps in the leaflet on page **23**. The words you need **do not** occur in the memorandum. **Use no more than two words for each gap**. The exercise begins with an example (**0**).

Example: | **0** | *no charge* | **0** |

MEMORANDUM

> **To:** Jane Smith – Marketing Manager
> **From:** Karen Jones – Information Officer
> **Subject:** School Visits
>
> Please can you make sure that all the following points are included in the information. First of all, it's worth mentioning that teachers don't have to pay if they want to have a look round Antley House before taking their class there. Also, they get 20% off when they take a group of more than 15.
>
> Most of what's in the house is more than 200 years old and worth a lot of money, so visitors aren't allowed to do the following:
>
> (1) Touch anything on show – lots of things would break easily.
> (2) Take their own pictures – there are postcards they can buy.
> (3) Take in big bags – they'll have to hand them in at the security desk as they go in. There have been some cases of people unintentionally knocking things over and breaking them.
> (4) Try to open blinds – it's meant to be quite dark in there so that the furniture doesn't get damaged. This shouldn't spoil their visit!
>
> Explain that we have to have these rules to stop the house from being damaged.

LEAFLET

Antley House – Advice for school parties

Teachers are urged to make a preliminary visit, for which there is **(0)** ..... , prior to arranging a school visit. There are **(62)** ..... rates for groups of 15 or more.

Many of the contents of Antley House **(63)** ..... the 17th century. Therefore, owing to the **(64)** ..... nature of the furniture and ornaments on display in this property, there are certain things which visitors are **(65)** ..... doing.

As many exhibits are extremely **(66)** ..... , visitors are asked to refrain from touching or handling anything. We regret that no **(67)** ..... is allowed by visitors inside the historic house. However, postcards are **(68)** ..... .Visitors will be asked **(69)** ..... large items at the security desk, **(70)** ..... Antley House. This is to stop furniture and ornaments from being **(71)** ..... damaged. We therefore advise school parties not to bring bags with them. Blinds are used in most rooms **(72)** ..... the furniture from fading caused **(73)** ..... . Please do not open them.

These measures are considered **(74)** ..... for the safekeeping of Antley House.

Part 6

For questions **75–80**, read the following text and then choose from the list **A–J** given below, the best phrase to fill each of the spaces. Write one letter (**A–J**) in the correct box on your answer sheet. Each correct phrase may only be used once. **Some of the suggested answers do not fit at all.** The exercise begins with an example (**0**).

Example:

0	J		0
			—

Blown Off Course

For the residents of the sleepy seaside town of Lowestoft, 3 September, 1965 was a day to remember. **(0)** ..... , when the wind began to blow, the sky darkened and an unusual cloud appeared. As it approached, people were astonished to see objects dropping onto the ground. **(75)** ..... blown off course by an unexpected storm. As townspeople ran for shelter from the rain, some even had birds landing on their heads. **(76)** ..... . All along the coast thousands of exhausted birds were falling out of the skies. This was the biggest migration of birds ever recorded in Britain. **(77)** ..... , one birdwatcher recorded a staggering total of more than 30,000 birds.

Each autumn, millions of migrating birds leave Scandinavia. **(78)** ..... , they ran into thick clouds and heavy rain. The birds were disoriented by the bad weather. Many became exhausted and fell into the sea, but others pressed on. **(79)** ..... to the delight of local birdwatchers. Fortunately, weather conditions rapidly improved and, after resting and feeding, the birds departed south.

To observe such migrants, you need to watch out for high pressure over Scandinavia, combined with unsettled weather over the eastern part of the British Isles and an onshore wind. **(80)** ..... head towards the east coast soon after dawn and, with luck, you will be rewarded with an unforgettable experience.

A This phenomenon was not confined to Lowestoft
B The area was crowded with birdwatchers
C On this occasion, crossing the North Sea
D These giant 'raindrops' were, in fact, migrating birds
E Those were the only birds to survive
F If these conditions are in place during the evening
G The next day when the wind dropped
H These lucky survivors landed on the British coast
I Once the weather had altered sufficiently

J It all started in the early afternoon

PAPER 4   LISTENING (approximately 45 minutes)

Part 1

You will hear a talk given by a woman who is a successful climber. For questions **1–10**, complete the sentences.

You will hear the recording twice.

MOUNTAIN CLIMBER

On her expedition, she became aware of the feelings of

| *and* | **1** | connected with mountaineering.

She had previously taken part in several so-called | **2**

She found the | **3** | for climbing Everest particularly hard.

She was particularly worried about the | **4**

she would have to climb through.

She says that you cannot take any of the | **5**

of life with you on Everest.

On her first trip there, she regretted taking | **6** | with her.

When she climbed Everest, she left her | **7**

after a certain point.

She says you mustn't waste | **8**

or fuel when you're on the mountain.

When they reached the top, they had a sensation of | **9**

Her book about climbing Everest is called | **10**

Part 2

You will hear a radio music presenter talking about his job. For questions **11–19**, complete the sentences.

Listen very carefully as you will hear the recording ONCE only.

MUSIC PRESENTER

He got a degree in [**11**] from university.

On leaving university, he began a career in [**12**]

His first experience of broadcasting was at a [**13**] station.

When he first tried to work in radio professionally,
he got a lot of [**14**]

One station invited him to attend some [**15**]

The programme he presents usually lasts for [**16**]

When he arrives, he starts by [**17**]

Then he works out what the [**18**]
and running order of his programme will be.

After lunch he looks through the [**19**]

Part 3

You will hear part of an interview with someone who founded a magazine. For questions **20–25**, choose the correct answer **A**, **B**, **C** or **D**.

You will hear the recording twice.

20 How was *Time Out* unlike other publications in 1968?

    A   It was written by one person.
    B   Information was more accurate.
    C   It had a comprehensive list of events.
    D   It was in the form of a magazine.

21 What experience did Tony have of publishing?

    A   He had worked for *What's On.*
    B   He had written numerous articles.
    C   He had transformed an existing magazine.
    D   He had started a student magazine.

22 Why did Tony leave university?

    A   He wanted to go to France.
    B   He didn't have time to study.
    C   He had failed his French examinations.
    D   He had found an alternative career.

23 What led to the magazine becoming a weekly?

    A   some market research
    B   the quantity of information
    C   technical improvements
    D   external pressure

24 Why were the big publishers not interested in this type of magazine?

    A   It was popular with students.
    B   It was considered too expensive.
    C   It came out too frequently.
    D   It threatened their publications.

25 Compared to 1968, people who buy *Time Out* today are

    A   more intelligent and active.
    B   more likely to be parents.
    C   more or less the same age.
    D   more mature and professional.

Part 4

You will hear five short extracts in which different people are talking about things that have recently happened at work.

You will hear the recording twice. While you listen you must complete both tasks.

TASK ONE

For questions **26–30**, match the extracts with the situations, listed **A–H**.

A   receiving an unwelcome visitor

B   being unfairly blamed for something   **Speaker 1** ☐ 26

C   making a terrible mistake
                                             Speaker 2 ☐ 27
D   receiving an unexpected offer

E   doing something uncharacteristic   **Speaker 3** ☐ 28

F   resolving a misunderstanding
                                             Speaker 4 ☐ 29
G   avoiding an argument

H   changing an opinion of someone   **Speaker 5** ☐ 30

TASK TWO

For questions **31–35**, match the extracts with the feeling each speaker expresses, listed **A–H**.

A   amusement
                                             Speaker 1 ☐ 31
B   anger

C   guilt   **Speaker 2** ☐ 32

D   confusion
                                             Speaker 3 ☐ 33
E   resignation

F   shock   **Speaker 4** ☐ 34

G   suspicion
                                             Speaker 5 ☐ 35
H   sadness

PAPER 5   SPEAKING (15 minutes)

There are two examiners. One (the Interlocutor) conducts the test, providing you with the necessary materials and explaining what you have to do. The other examiner (the Assessor) is introduced to you, but then takes no further part in the interaction.

Part 1 (3 minutes)

The Interlocutor first asks you and your partner a few questions. You are then asked to find out some information about each other, on topics such as hobbies, interests, future plans, etc. You are then asked further questions by the Interlocutor.

Part 2 (4 minutes)

You are each given the opportunity to talk for about a minute, and to comment briefly after your partner has spoken.

The Interlocutor gives you a set of pictures and asks you to talk about them for about one minute. It is important to listen carefully to the Interlocutor's instructions. The Interlocutor then asks your partner a question about your pictures and your partner responds briefly.

You are then given another set of pictures to look at. Your partner talks about these pictures for about one minute. This time the Interlocutor asks you a question about your partner's pictures and you respond briefly.

Part 3 (approximately 4 minutes)

In this part of the test you and your partner are asked to talk together. The Interlocutor places a new set of pictures on the table between you. This stimulus provides the basis for a discussion. The Interlocutor explains what you have to do.

Part 4 (approximately 4 minutes)

The Interlocutor asks some further questions, which leads to a more general discussion of what you have talked about in Part 3. You may comment on your partner's answers if you wish.

Test 2

PAPER 1   READING (1 hour 15 minutes)

Part 1

Answer questions **1–16** by referring to the newspaper interviews on page **31** about book reviews. Indicate your answers **on the separate answer sheet**.

For questions **1–16**, answer by choosing from publishers (**A–E**) on page **31**. Some of the choices may be required more than once.
Note: When more than one answer is required, these may be given **in any order**.

Which publisher(s)

say that some books succeed whether they are reviewed or not?	**1** .... **2** ....
mentions reviewers taking the opportunity to display their own expertise?	**3** ....
describes how good reviews can contribute to the commercial failure of a book?	**4** ....
says that writers and publishers do not react to negative reviews in the same way?	**5** ....
feels that certain books are frequently overlooked by reviewers?	**6** ....
talks about the sales of some books being stimulated by mixed reviews?	**7** ....
suggest that the length of a review may be more important to publishers than what it actually says?	**8** .... **9** ....
refer to the influence of reviews written by well-known people?	**10** .... **11** ....
says the effect of reviews on sales does not have a regular pattern?	**12** ....
talks of the satisfaction publishers feel at seeing their own views confirmed in a review?	**13** ....
mention reviews being a crucial form of promotion?	**14** .... **15** ....
believes there has been an improvement in the standard of book reviews?	**16** ....

DO REVIEWS SELL BOOKS?

**We asked five leading British publishers about the effect of the reviews
of a book on its commercial success. Here is what they said.**

Publisher A

Reviews are absolutely key for publishers – the first part of
the newspaper we turn to. The Book Marketing Council
found some years ago that when questioned on why they had
bought a particular book, more people cited reviews than any
other prompting influence (advertisements, word of mouth,
bookshop display, etc.).

Authors' responses to reviews are slightly different from
publishers'. Both are devastated by no reviews, but
publishers are usually more equable about the bad reviews,
judging that column inches are what matter and that a
combination of denunciation and ecstatic praise can actually
create sales as readers decide to judge for themselves.

Publishers probably get the most pleasure from a review
which precisely echoes their own response to a book – they
are often the first 'reader'.

Publisher B

While publishers and the press fairly obviously have a
common interest in the nature of book review pages, one also
needs to remember that their requirements substantially
differ: a newspaper or magazine needs to provide its readers
with appropriately entertaining material; a publishing house
wants to see books, preferably its own, reviewed, preferably
favourably.

Without any question, book reviewing is 'better' – more
diverse, less elitist – than 40 years ago, when I began reading
review pages. That said, there is still a long-grumbled-about
tendency to neglect the book medium read by a majority –
namely paperbacks. The weekly roundups aren't really
adequate even if conscientiously done. And even original
paperbacks only rarely receive serious coverage.

But publishers shouldn't complain too much. Like readers
and writers, they need reviews, which after all are an
economical way of getting a book and an author known.
There is no question that a lively account of a new book by
a trusted name can generate sales – even more if there are
several of them. Fame is what puts a book into the hands of
readers.

Publisher C

Reviews are the oxygen of literary publishing; without them,
we would be cut off from an essential life-source. Because the
books we publish are generally not by 'brand-name' authors,
whose books sell with or without reviews, and because we
seldom advertise, we depend on the space given to our books
by literary editors.

When the reviews are favourable, of course, they are worth
infinitely more than any advertisement. The reader knows
that the good review is not influenced by the publisher's
marketing budget: it is the voice of reason, and there is no
doubt that it helps to sell books. Publishers themselves often
claim that they look for size rather than content in reviews.

The actual effect of reviews on sales is the inscrutable heart
of the whole business. Good reviews can launch a book and
a career and occasionally lift sales into the stratosphere: but
never entirely on their own. There has to be some fusion
with other elements – a word-of-mouth network of
recommendation, a robust response from the book trade,
clever marketing.

Publisher D

The relationship in Britain between publishing and
reviewing? I wish I knew! In the United States it's simple: the
New York Times can make or break a book with a single
review. Here, though, the people in the bookshops often
don't appear to take much notice of them.

It sometimes takes 20 years of consistently outstanding
reviews for people to start reading a good writer's work. Yet
some of the most dismally received books, or books not yet
reviewed, are the biggest sellers of all. So it's all very
unpredictable, though non-fiction is less so.

Mind you, non-fiction does allow reviewers to indulge
themselves by telling us what they know about the subject of
the book under review rather than about the book itself.

Publisher E

Of course, all publishers and all writers dream of long,
uniformly laudatory reviews. But do they sell books? I once
published a biography. The reviews were everything I could
have craved. The book was a flop – because everyone thought
that, by reading the lengthy reviews, they need not buy the
book.

Does the name of the reviewer make a difference? Thirty
years ago, if certain reviewers praised a book, the public
seemed to take note and obey their recommendations. These
days, it is as much the choice of an unexpected reviewer, or
the sheer power or wit or originality of the review, which
urges the prospective buyer into the bookshop.

Part 2

For questions **17–22**, choose which of the paragraphs **A–G** on page **33** fit into the numbered gaps in the following magazine article. There is one extra paragraph, which does not fit in any of the gaps. Indicate your answers **on the separate answer sheet**.

Chewing gum culture

It's fashionable, classless and Americans chew 12 million sticks of it a day.
Discover how an ancient custom became big business.

Chewing gum contains fewer than ten calories per stick, but it is classified as a food and must therefore conform to the standards of the American Food and Drug Administration.

Today's gum is largely synthetic, with added pine resins and softeners which help to hold the flavour and improve the texture.

17	

American colonists followed the example of the Amero-Indians of New England and chewed the resin that formed on spruce trees when the bark was cut. Lumps of spruce for chewing were sold in the eastern United States in the early 1800s making it the first commercial chewing gum in the country.

Modern chewing gum has its origins in the late 1860s with the discovery of *chicle*, a milky substance obtained from the sapodilla tree of the Central American rainforest.

18	

Yet repeated attempts to cultivate sapodilla commercially have failed. As the chewing gum market has grown, synthetic alternatives have had to be developed.

19	

Most alarming is the unpleasant little *chicle* fly that likes to lodge its eggs in the tapper's ears and nose.

Braving these hazards, barefooted and with only a rope and an axe, an experienced *chiclero* will shin a mature tree in minutes to cut a path in the bark for the white sap to flow down to a bag below.

20	

Yet, punishing though this working environment is, the remaining *chicleros* fear for their livelihood.

Not so long ago, the United States alone imported 7,000 tonnes of *chicle* a year from Central America. Last year just 200 tonnes were tapped in the whole of Mexico's Yucatan peninsula. As chewing gum sales have soared, so the manufacturers have turned to synthetics to reduce costs and meet demands.

21	

Plaque acid, which forms when we eat, causes this. Our saliva, which neutralises the acid and supplies minerals such as calcium, phosphate and fluoride, is the body's natural defence. Gum manufacturers say 20 minutes of chewing can increase your salivary flow.

22	

In addition, one hundred and thirty-seven square kilometres of America is devoted entirely to producing the mint that is used in the two most popular chewing gums in the world.

A Gum made from this resulted in a smoother, more satisfying and more elastic chew, and soon a whole industry was born based on this product.

B Meanwhile, the world's gum producers are finding ingenious ways of marketing their products. In addition to all the claims made for gum – it helps you relax, peps you up and eases tension (soldiers during both world wars were regularly supplied with gum) – gum's greatest claim is that it reduces tooth decay.

C Research continues on new textures and flavours. Glycerine and other vegetable oil products are now used to blend the gum base. Most new flavours are artificial – but some flavours still need natural assistance.

D This was not always the case, though. The ancient Greeks chewed a gum-like resin obtained from the bark of the mastic tree, a shrub found mainly in Greece and Turkey. Grecian women, especially, favoured mastic gum to clean their teeth and sweeten their breath.

E Each *chiclero* must carry the liquid on his back to a forest camp, where it is boiled until sticky and made into bricks. Life at the camp is no picnic either, with a monotonous and often deficient maize-based diet washed down by a local alcohol distilled from sugar cane.

F The *chicleros* grease their hands and arms to prevent the sticky gum sticking to them. The gum is then packed into a wooden mould, pressed down firmly, initialled and dated ready for collection and export.

G Today the few remaining *chicle* gatherers, *chicleros*, eke out a meagre and dangerous living, trekking for miles to tap scattered sapodilla in near-100% humidity. Conditions are appalling: highly poisonous snakes lurk ready to pounce and insects abound.

Part 3

Read the following newspaper article about an expedition and answer questions 23–29 on page 35. **On your answer sheet**, indicate the letter **A**, **B**, **C** or **D** against the number of each question. Give only one answer to each question.

An awfully big adventure

The Taklamakan Desert in western China is one of the last unexplored places on earth. It is also one of the most dangerous. Charles Blackmore crossed it, and lived to tell the tale.

There are very few big adventures left and very few heroes. Children's stories used to specialise in them – courageous explorers with sunburnt, leathery skin and eyes narrowed by straining to see into far horizons on their journeys into the unknown. These days you no longer find such people in fiction, let alone in real life. Or so I thought until I met Charles Blackmore.

Blackmore's great adventure consisted of leading an expedition across one of the last unexplored places on earth, the Taklamakan Desert in western China. Its name means 'once entered you never come out', but local people call it the Desert of Death. He recalled the dangers and exhilaration of that amazing trek, in the calm atmosphere of his family home.

The team he led was composed of four Britons (one of them the party's medical officer), an American photographer, four Chinese (all experts on the area), 30 camels and six camel handlers. It later turned out that the camel handlers had never worked with camels before, but were long-distance lorry drivers: a misunderstanding that could have cost everyone their lives and certainly jeopardised the expedition's success. This mixed bunch set out to cross 1,200 kilometres of the world's least hospitable desert and Charles Blackmore has written a mesmerising account of their journey.

At the time, he was about to leave the Army after 14 happy years. He launched the expedition for fun, to fill a gap in his life, to prove something. 'I had always assumed I'd spend my whole life in the Army. I had been offered promotion but suddenly I felt I wanted to see who Charles Blackmore really was, outside all that. It was a tremendous gamble. Tina, my wife, was very worried that I wouldn't come back as nobody had ever done that route; we went into it blind. In the event, it took 59 days to cross from west to east, and the desert was very kind to us.'

Anyone reading his extraordinary account of that crossing will wonder at the use of the word 'kind'. The team suffered unspeakable hardships: dysentery; extremes of temperature; severe thirst and dehydration; the loss of part of their precious water supply. 'But', Blackmore explains, 'when we were at the limits of our own endurance and the camels had gone without water for seven days, we managed to find some. We didn't experience the Taklamakan's legendary sandstorms. And we never hit the raw, biting desert cold that would have totally immobilised us. That's not to say that we weren't fighting against hurdles the whole time. The fine sand got into everything, especially blisters and wounds. The high dunes were torture to climb, for us and for the heavily laden camels, which often rolled over onto us.

'What drove me on more than anything else was the need to survive. We had no contingency plan. Neither our budget nor time allowed one. No aircraft ever flew over us. Once we got into the sandhills we were completely on our own.

'I knew I had the mental stamina for the trip but I was very scared of my physical ability to do it. I remember day one – we sat at the edge of the desert and it was such an inferno that you couldn't breathe. I thought, "We've got to do it now!" At that moment I was a very scared man.'

If it was like that at the beginning, how did they feel towards the end? 'When you've walked for 1,000 kilometres you're not going to duck out. You've endured so much; you've got so much behind you. We were very thin, but very muscular and sinewy despite our physical exhaustion. My body was well-toned and my legs were like pistons. I could walk over anything.'

Midway through the book, Blackmore went on to describe lying in the desert gazing up at a full moon, thinking of his family. How conscious was he of the ordeal it must have been for them? 'Inside me there's someone trying to find peace with himself. When I have doubts about myself now, I go back to the image of the desert and think, well, we managed to pull that together. As a personal achievement, I feel prouder of that expedition than of anything else I've done. Yet in terms of a lifetime's achievement, I think of my family and the happiness we share – against that yardstick, the desert does not measure up, does not compare.'

Has Charles Blackmore found peace? 'I yearn for the challenge – for the open spaces – the resolve of it all. We were buoyed up by the sense of purpose. I find it difficult now to be part of the uniformity of modern life.'

23   Meeting Charles Blackmore changed the writer's opinion about

    A   the content of children's fiction.
    B   the nature of desert exploration.
    C   the existence of traditional heroes.
    D   the activities of explorers.

24   When the expedition members set off, some of the group

    A   posed an unexpected risk.
    B   disagreed with each other.
    C   were doubtful of success.
    D   went on ahead of the others.

25   Blackmore had decided to set up the expedition because

    A   he was certain he could complete it.
    B   he wanted to write a book.
    C   his aims in life had changed.
    D   his self-confidence was low.

26   Which of the following best describes the team's experience of the desert?

    A   They were not able to have enough rest.
    B   It presented continual difficulties.
    C   They sometimes could not make any progress at all.
    D   It was worse than they had expected.

27   Which of the following did Blackmore experience during the trip?

    A   frustration at the lack of funding
    B   regret about the lack of planning
    C   realisation that they would receive no help
    D   fear that he would let his companions down

28   According to Blackmore, what enabled him to finish the expedition?

    A   his strength of will
    B   his physical preparation
    C   his closeness to his family
    D   his understanding of the desert

29   How does Blackmore feel now that the expedition is over?

    A   tired but pleased to be home
    B   regretful about his family's distress
    C   unsure of his ability to repeat it
    D   unsettled by the experience

Part 4

Answer questions **30–45** by referring to the magazine article on pages **37–38** about different jobs. Indicate your answers **on the separate answer sheet**.

For questions **30–45**, choose your answers from the people (**A–F**) on pages **37–38**. Some of the choices may be required more than once.

Note: When more than one answer is required, these may be given **in any order**.

According to the article, which person/people

starts planning his/her schedule on arrival at work?   **30** ....

is irritated by the attitude of some people?   **31** ....

needs to attract new clients as part of his/her job?   **32** ....

mentions ambitions for the future?   **33** ....

relies on intuition in making decisions?   **34** ....

mentions reviewing his/her work for accuracy?   **35** ....

has scheduled breaks?   **36** ....

spend time discussing the most effective means of promotion?   **37** .... **38** ....

makes a point of being accessible?   **39** ....

makes an effort to find out about new regulations in his/her   **40** ....
profession?

works under the pressure of fixed completion times?   **41** ....

emphasise that their jobs have both artistic and financial   **42** .... **43** ....
aspects?

produces reports of varying levels of detail?   **44** ....

does not work unless he/she feels in the best of health?   **45** ....

Careers

Six people talk about their typical working day.

A Credit Card Executive

I get up at 6 am to arrive at the office around 7.30 am. I manage all the customer development programmes for our regular credit card users. My responsibilities include the launch and management of the Membership Rewards scheme in the major European markets. I have to keep in touch with existing card users, acquire new ones and build relationships with partner companies.

I use the first 45 minutes to organise my day and then I respond to any e-mail messages. I manage all the advertising for the membership programme across Europe, so I meet with our marketing staff and the advertising agencies to establish a strategy and work on future developments. I have meetings scheduled for most of the day, but at all other times I make sure I keep my door open for anyone to come and ask me questions.

There are nine customer service units around Europe and I have to travel to the different markets once or twice a week to discuss issues that come up. When I'm in London, I leave work between 6.30 pm and 7.00 pm.

B Record Company Executive

I get to work for 10.00 am and go through the post – between ten and twenty demonstration tapes a day, letters from producers and information about concerts, as well as invoices from session musicians and studios. The phone starts ringing at about 10.30 am – producers, publishers and so on, and there are meetings arranged throughout the day to talk about campaigns or projects for a particular artist. This might involve the press, marketing and the managing director.

When I listen to demo tapes I am very aware that people are bringing in their life's work, so I try to be constructive. I instinctively know if the sound is appropriate for our record label. Once I've signed a band, we start on the first album – choosing the songs, producer, and additional musicians. Then I have to communicate my vision of the album to the rest of the company for marketing and selling. I also oversee budgets and spending.

I leave work at 7.00 pm at the earliest and most evenings I go to gigs – sometimes I see as many as five new groups a night. Sometimes after a gig I'll visit an artist in the studio. Most of my socialising revolves around my work. I often don't get home until 1.00 am – when I put on a record to help me wind down.

C Sales Director

I get up at 8.00 am and drive to work to arrive at 9.30 am. I open the post, look through the diary to check if we're going to see any clients that day, then wait and see who turns up.

I love taking people round the showrooms – there's nothing better than reaching an agreement with someone, selling them a piece of furniture and knowing it's going to a good home. We sell antiques from £1,000 to £6,000 and buy from the London salerooms, country house sales, our private clients and overseas.

A lot of what we buy needs restoration. We have a full-time restorer in the shop, and I spend a lot of time liaising with gilders, picture framers and paper repairers. I read the *Antiques Trade Gazette* while I drink coffee at odd moments, to keep in touch with what's going on in the business, and I often pop into the Victoria and Albert museum to compare furniture.

I do the accounts one day every month and every three months I do the tax returns. At 5.30 pm I go home. It usually takes me about an hour to switch off.

D Air Traffic Controller

I work a set shift pattern, and when I'm on an early shift I leave the house at 6.00 am. At 7.00 am I relieve the night shift and take over one of the four control positions in the tower.

We have a rotating timetable, which means that I work for about an hour and a half at one of the stations, go off for half an hour and then come back to a different station. The air traffic controllers, a supervisor and the watch manager all sit near to each other and work as a team, controlling the aircraft movements.

In winter we deal with about 1,000 movements a day, and even more in summer. Night shifts are much quieter, and I usually get a chance to read up on new air traffic requirements between 12 and 4.00 am.

It's important to be really switched on in this job, so even if I'm only a bit under the weather I have no qualms about being off sick. I find the work quite stressful and it can take a while to wind down at the end of a shift. Eventually I'd like to be watch manager, and then maybe even general manager of the airport.

E Shop Manager

If I'm on an early shift, I leave the house by 8.00 am. The first thing I do is get the electronic point-of-sale system up and running.

I always make sure there's someone to watch the till and I co-ordinate people's lunches and breaks. I spend the morning helping customers, finding and ordering books for them. I enjoy serving customers, although it can be a bit annoying if they come in waving reviews and expect you to run around gathering a pile of books for them.

Between 2.00 pm and 4.00 pm most weekdays, publishers' reps come into the shop and I spend some time discussing new titles for the months ahead. I have to consider how many, if any, of a particular title the shop is likely to sell. When we want to feature a new title, it's essential that I make sure it's delivered in time.

The early shift finishes at 5.45 pm. Two days a week I do a late shift, and then I close down the computer system, lock up and go home.

F Financial Analyst

I listen to the news at 7.00 am, then get up and take a taxi to arrive at work at 8.45 am. First I get in touch with our freelance reporters to find out what is happening in the region I'm responsible for.

I assess financial risk for multi-national companies operating abroad, so it is my job to try to warn clients well in advance of anything that could go wrong in that country. I provide three services: an on-line executive preview, or newsflash; a security forecast, which is an extended preview plus a forecast for the next six months; and a travel information security guide.

From 9.15 am to 9.30 am I meet with our editors to discuss the stories I'm going to follow. My first executive preview has to be on-line by 10.00 am and my second deadline is 11.00 am, so I have to be quick chasing up stories. I type them, send them through to my editor, who edits and approves them, then I re-check and make any necessary alterations before they go through the system.

I travel to Africa about three times a year, to report on specific events or just to keep up with what is happening. I leave work at around 6.00 pm. It's quite difficult to switch off, and most evenings I'm still awake at 1.00 am.

PAPER 2   WRITING (2 hours)

Part 1

1 You are the social organiser at Whitecross College in Britain, where you are studying. The local newspaper has recently published an article criticising the students at the college. As a result, your Principal has decided to organise an Open Day at the College, and has asked you to write a letter for publication in the newspaper, responding to the article and publicising the Open Day.

Read the article below on which your Principal has made some notes, together with the Principal's memo on page **40**. Then, **using the information appropriately**, write a letter to the editor of the newspaper, apologising to local residents and encouraging people to come to the Open Day.

LOCAL RESIDENTS FURIOUS: STUDENTS IN TROUBLE AGAIN

Residents living near Whitecross College are again complaining about the behaviour of students from the college. Mrs Jones, who lives nearby, complained, 'We are woken up time and time again late at night by noisy groups of students. No wonder the college exam results are so poor!' Her neighbour, Robert Adams, added: 'They stand around in large groups during the day as well, blocking the pavement and dropping litter everywhere. Don't they do any work at all? Doesn't the college organise a social programme for them?'

---

must apologise

not true!

extremely varied

```
                        MEMO

    TO:     The Social Organiser

    FROM:   The Principal

    RE:     College Open Day,
            Saturday 11 October,
            10.30 am - 10.30 pm


    After the recent newspaper article, we must make
    local people more aware of all the good things that
    happen here - our excellent facilities, our first-
    class exam results and our varied social programme.
    I've made a few notes about plans for the day.
    Please give information about these in a letter to
    the newspaper. Your letter should include a brief
    apology to local residents, and encourage people to
    come to the Open Day. Here are some of the things
    the day will include:

    • international barbecue.

    • college concert. Give details.

    • afternoon Sports Challenge - tennis and football
      against local teams.

    • chance to try our computer centre and language
      laboratory.

    • display of photographs of college
      activities - cultural, environmental, etc.
```

Now write a **letter** to the editor of the local newspaper as requested by the Principal (approximately 250 words). You should use your own words as far as possible. You do not need to include postal addresses.

Part 2

Choose **one** of the following writing tasks. Your answer should follow exactly the instructions given. Write approximately 250 words.

2   You would like to start a monthly magazine in English for students at the college where you are studying. You have decided to send a proposal to the college Principal asking for permission and financial support. Your proposal must include the following:

  • why you want to start the magazine
  • what the first issue would include
  • what support and financial help you need from the college.

Write your **proposal**.

3   While staying in an international youth hostel, you see the following announcement in its magazine:

COMPETITION

Should we travel alone, with friends or with family?

What are the benefits of **each** and are there any disadvantages?

Write and tell us what you think.

We will publish the best entries in next month's magazine and the winner will receive a mountain bike.

Write your **competition entry**.

4   An English magazine has a weekly column called *It'll Cost The Earth*. As part of their worldwide investigation into environmental issues, they have asked you to write a report for them, addressing the following questions:

  • What is being done to cut down on the use of energy and natural resources in your village, town or city?
  • How successful are these measures?
  • What more could be done?

Write your **report**.

5   Someone in your department has applied for a job in the marketing department of a multinational company and you have been asked to write a character reference for the applicant. You should indicate how long and in what capacity you have worked with this person, comment on his or her business skills and experience **and** mention any additional personal qualities that you think might be relevant to a marketing position.

Write your **character reference**.

PAPER 3   ENGLISH IN USE (1 hour 30 minutes)

Part 1

For questions **1–15**, read the text below and then decide which word on page **43** best fits each space. Put the letter you choose for each question in the correct box on your answer sheet. The exercise begins with an example (**0**).

Example: | 0 | A | | 0 |

Sports Photography

Sport as a spectacle, and photography as a way of recording action, have developed together. At the **(0)** ..... of the 20th century, Edward Muybridge was experimenting with photographs of movement. His pictures of a runner **(1)** ..... in every history of photography. Another milestone was when the scientist/photographer Harold Edgerton **(2)** ..... the limits of photographic technology with his study of a **(3)** ..... of milk hitting the surface of a dish of milk. Another advance was the development of miniature cameras in the late 1920s which made it possible for sports photographers to **(4)** ..... their cumbersome cameras behind.

The significance of television as a transmitter of sport has **(5)** ..... the prospects of still photographers. All those people who watch a sports event on TV, with all its movement and action, **(6)** ..... the still image as a reminder of the game. The **(7)** ..... majority of people do not actually **(8)** ..... sports events, but see them through the eyes of the media. And when they look at sports photography, they look not so much for a **(9)** ..... of the event as for emotions and relationships with which they can **(10)** ..... .

Looking back, we can see how **(11)** ..... sports photography has changed. **(12)** ..... sports photographers were as interested in the stories behind the sport as in the sport itself. Contemporary sports photography **(13)** ..... the glamour of sport, the colour and the action. But the best sports photographers today still do more than **(14)** ..... tell the story of the event. They **(15)** ..... in a single dramatic moment the real emotions of the participants.

0 (A) turn   B   opening   C   origin   D   introduction

1 A   exhibit   B   show   C   feature   D   demonstrate

2 A   enlarged   B   extended   C   prolonged   D   spread

3 A   splash   B   drop   C   dash   D   drip

4 A   put   B   keep   C   lay   D   leave

5 A   improved   B   aided   C   benefited   D   assisted

6 A   choose   B   value   C   praise   D   cheer

7 A   high   B   wide   C   main   D   vast

8 A   visit   B   attend   C   follow   D   meet

9 A   preservation   B   store   C   mark   D   record

10 A   identify   B   share   C   unite   D   join

11 A   highly   B   radically   C   extremely   D   severely

12 A   Initial   B   First   C   Early   D   Primary

13 A   outlines   B   signals   C   emphasises   D   forms

14 A   simply   B   alone   C   singly   D   only

15 A   seize   B   grasp   C   capture   D   secure

Part 2

For questions **16–30**, complete the following article by writing each missing word in the correct box on your answer sheet. **Use only one word for each space**. The exercise begins with an example (**0**).

Example:

0	*what*	0

Traffic Jams are Nothing New

In the age before the motor car, **(0)** ..... was travelling in London like? Photographs taken 100 years ago showing packed streets indicate that it was much the **(16)** ..... as it is now. Commuters who choose the car to get to work probably travel at **(17)** ..... average speed of 17 kph from their homes **(18)** ..... the suburbs to offices in the centre. **(19)** ..... is virtually the same speed that they **(20)** ..... have travelled at in a horse and carriage a century ago.

As towns and cities grow, **(21)** ..... does traffic, whether in the form of the horse and carriage **(22)** ..... the modern motor car. It would seem that, wherever **(23)** ..... are people who need to go somewhere, they would **(24)** ..... be carried than walk or pedal. The photographs show that, in terms **(25)** ..... congestion and speed, traffic in London hasn't changed over the past 100 years. London has had traffic jams ever **(26)** ..... it became a huge city. It is only the vehicles that have changed.

However, although London had traffic congestion long **(27)** ..... the car came along, the age of the horse produced little unpleasantness apart **(28)** ..... the congestion. Today, exhaust fumes create dangerous smogs that cause breathing problems **(29)** ..... a great many people. Such problems could be reduced **(30)** ..... many of us avoided jams by using bicycles or taking a brisk walk to school or work.

Part 3

In **most** lines of the following text, there is **one** unnecessary word. It is either grammatically incorrect or does not fit in with the sense of the text. For each numbered line **31–46**, find this word and then write it in the box on your answer sheet. **Some lines are correct**. Indicate these lines with a tick (✔) in the box. The exercise begins with two examples (**0**) and (**00**).

Examples:

0	✔	0
00	*all*	0

Sesame

0   Sesame was one of the earliest herbs known to the world. There is some

00 disagreement among all the authorities as to the exact place of origin of this

31 ancient herb; it may only have been Africa, Afghanistan or the East Indies.

32 It is then mentioned in Sanskrit literature and Egyptian scripts, as well as

33 in old Hebrew writings. Cleopatra is supposed to have been used sesame

34 oil as a skin beautifier. Sesame used to grow in the wild, but recently has

35 been grown up as an important crop in many parts of the world. It grows to

36 both three or four feet high and has white flowers that are followed by seeds

37 which produce oil, high in protein and mineral content. A product of sesame

38 seeds is an edible cream known as tahini, which has had the consistency of

39 honey and is extremely popular in Middle Eastern and Greek food. Tahini is

40 the principal ingredient in a popular sweet called halva. When being chilled

41 and cut into small blocks it makes as an agreeable accompaniment to black

42 coffee. Sesame seed and honey bars are tasty sweets found out in cake

43 shops and delicatessens. Sesame meal, which is ground sesame seed, is

44 obtained from health-food shops and is increasingly found in some of bigger

45 supermarkets. As it is so high itself in protein, vegetarians use large quantities

46 of it in their daily diet. In fact therefore, anything using sesame is nutritious as
well as delicious.

Part 4

For questions **47–61**, read the two texts on pages **46** and **47**. Use the words in the boxes to the right of the texts to form **one** word that fits in the same numbered space in the text. Write the new word in the correct box on your answer sheet. The exercise begins with an example (**0**).

Example:

0	*celebration*	0

REVIEW OF A COOKERY BOOK

The Cook's Garden

The Cook's Garden is a **(0)** ..... of the fruits, vegetables and herbs of the garden. It is filled with enthusiasm for both gardening and cooking and contains over 300 delicious recipes.

Sheridan Rogers emphasises **(47)** ..... of ingredients and **(48)** ..... of preparation in her cooking. There are both traditional and innovative recipes, all of which make **(49)** ..... use of ingredients which are in season. In order to **(50)** ..... a constant supply of ingredients, Sheridan includes advice and **(51)** ..... handy tips for growing fruit and vegetables.

The illustrations in *The Cook's Garden* are by Sheridan's sister, Skye. Her **(52)** ..... pastel drawings show the colour and beauty of familiar everyday fruit and vegetables as well as the more exotic **(53)** ..... .

(0)	**CELEBRATE**
(47)	FRESH
(48)	SIMPLE
(49)	CREATE
(50)	SURE
(51)	NUMBER
(52)	DELIGHT
(53)	VARY

46

COLLEGE ADVERTISEMENT

The Facts about Higher Education at Deacon College

- All our courses are approved and **(54)** ..... by the University of Dayton.
- Our range of programmes and choice of specialist subjects has been developed to meet the **(55)** ..... of our students and their **(56)** ..... employers.
- Our students have a very high pass rate – 98% completed their courses **(57)** ..... , with nearly a third progressing to a degree.

Why Study at Deacon College?

- You can choose a programme at an appropriate level from a wide **(58)** ..... of subjects.
- Your **(59)** ..... are all qualified professionals who are also committed and enthusiastic.
- If you live within reasonable **(60)** ..... travelling distance of the college you may benefit **(61)** ..... , since it can be more expensive to study away from home.

(54)	VALID
(55)	REQUIRE
(56)	PROSPECT
(57)	SUCCESS
(58)	CHOOSE
(59)	LECTURE
(60)	DAY
(61)	FINANCE

Part 5

For questions **62–74**, read the following note from a Directors' meeting and use the information in it to complete the numbered gaps in the memorandum on page **49**. The words you need **do not** occur in the note. **Use no more than two words for each gap**. The exercise begins with an example (**0**).

Example:

0	*inform you*	0

NOTE

Tim

Could you circulate a memo to all staff to let them know that we made up our minds at the Directors' meeting last week to have the office done up? We've now hired a firm to do the work and they're probably going to begin on the 14th. They reckon they'll probably need three weeks to do the job – life will be difficult, but there's no way we can get round this. While it's going on, the staff will have to work as normal. Tell them we're sorry if this causes them any trouble but we hope that it'll put them out as little as possible. Also say we'll be very glad of their co-operation and point out that when the work is finished, we are absolutely sure that the office environment will be much more pleasant. Oh, and mention that between now and then, if there are any colours they'd especially like, they should feel free to tell us.

MEMORANDUM

> **To:**   All Staff
>
> **From:** Tim Trout – Assistant to the Directors
>
> I am writing to **(0)** ..... of the **(62)** ..... taken at the Directors' meeting last week to **(63)** ..... the offices. A firm has been contracted to carry out this work, with the 14th May as the expected **(64)** ..... . They have **(65)** ..... that the work will take three weeks – this will involve some disruption, which I am afraid is totally **(66)** ..... . While the work is in **(67)** ..... all departments will continue to operate normally. The Directors would like to **(68)** ..... any problems that may be caused and hope that there will be only the **(69)** ..... inconvenience to you. They would greatly **(70)** ..... your co-operation in this matter and they have no **(71)** ..... that, on completion of the work, you will all be pleased to work in much more attractive **(72)** ..... . In the meantime, should you have any particular **(73)** ..... regarding colours, please do not **(74)** ..... put them forward.

Part 6

For questions **75–80**, read the following text and then choose from the list **A–J** given below, the best phrase to fill each of the spaces. Write one letter (**A–J**) in the correct box on your answer sheet. Each correct phrase may only be used once. **Some of the suggested answers do not fit at all.** The exercise begins with an example (**0**).

Example:

0	J	0

The Origin of Language

Over the centuries, language has enabled humans to share complex information. This wondrous ability eventually gave us the power **(0)** ..... . Imagine if people couldn't pass on certain types of information, such as what is required for building a wheel, without having **(75)** ..... . The concept might even die out and have to be re-invented by each new generation. With language, the concept of a wheel can spread very fast, and the original idea can be modified and improved on, time and again, until people are able **(76)** ..... . Nobody knows how the human ability **(77)** ..... . There are many different yet interesting theories. Some linguists think it came about because of people's need to co-operate with each other in order to hunt large animals. A group of humans communicating with each other would have a better chance of killing a large, potentially dangerous animal such as a mammoth. Other linguists believe that language stems from a desire **(78)** ..... . They see it as a re-enforcement of physical gesture. And others again attribute speech to the same spark of creativity that caused our distant ancestors **(79)** ..... . Most linguists, however, now believe that it is an innate ability, a natural result of the development of the human brain, much like the spider's natural ability to spin webs or the dolphin's ability **(80)** ..... .

A   to support this theory developed
B   to use language originated
C   to use high-pitched sounds to judge distances
D   to draw animals on cave walls
E   to learn any language perfectly
F   to manipulate and control people
G   to develop wheels with tyres and spokes
H   to laboriously demonstrate the technique
I   to express their ideas in words

J   to dominate the world

PAPER 4   LISTENING (approximately 45 minutes)

Part 1

You will hear a guide speaking to tourists who are visiting some Roman remains. For questions **1–9**, fill in the missing information.

You will hear the recording twice.

TOUR OF ROMAN REMAINS

pm – Visit to Roman _____ **1**

Romans came to area in AD _____ **2**

Built forts in region to _____ **3**

In 1201, people began to search for _____ **4**

In the early 19th century, excavators made some _____ **5**

Since 1934, archaeological digs have taken place once _____ **6**

First half of the museum shows the _____ **7**

Second half of museum shows different aspects of _____ **8**

On site: Watch out for loose stones and _____ **9**

Part 2

You will hear part of a radio programme in which someone is talking about a competition for choirs, or groups of singers. For questions **10–17**, fill in the missing information.

Listen very carefully as you will hear the recording ONCE only.

Competition held every [   ] **10**

3 categories: – Youth Choir

– [   ] **11** Choir

– Single Voice Choir

Choir sends in [   ] **12**

Auditions held from [   ] **13**

Competition televised from [   ] **14** stage onwards.

Choirs usually [   ] **15** when there are TV cameras.

Winner of each category receives a special [   ] **16**

Choir of the year also wins £1000 to buy [   ] **17**

Part 3

You will hear a radio discussion about an office practice called 'hot desking'. For questions **18–25**, complete the sentences.

You will hear the recording twice.

Peter likes 'hot desking' because it offers him [| **18**]

in the way he works.

Lois thinks that 'hot desking' creates a more [| **19**] atmosphere.

Peter thinks certain problems may be avoided if the office is [| **20**]

Lois has done [| **21**] which show that people are concerned about where they work.

Peter points to the fact that he can [| **22**] if he wishes.

Lois and Peter agree that [| **23**] in the workplace is important.

Lois thinks that young people learn important [| **24**] at work.

Peter points out that 'hot desking' actually helps create new [| **25**]

Part 4

You will hear five short extracts in which different people are talking about weekend activities.

You will hear the recording twice. While you listen you must complete both tasks.

TASK ONE

For questions **26–30**, match the extracts with the different activities, listed **A–H**.

A   mountaineering

B   going to the theatre   **Speaker 1** ⬚ 26

C   swimming in a lake   **Speaker 2** ⬚ 27

D   dining in a restaurant

E   watching a football match   **Speaker 3** ⬚ 28

F   fishing in a river   **Speaker 4** ⬚ 29

G   wandering around a market

H   attending a wedding   **Speaker 5** ⬚ 30

TASK TWO

For questions **31–35**, match the extracts with the opinion each speaker expresses about the activity, listed **A–H**.

A   disappointing   **Speaker 1** ⬚ 31

B   confusing   **Speaker 2** ⬚ 32

C   uneventful

D   overcrowded   **Speaker 3** ⬚ 33

E   frightening   **Speaker 4** ⬚ 34

F   unusual

G   amusing   **Speaker 5** ⬚ 35

H   exhausting

PAPER 5   SPEAKING (15 minutes for pairs of candidates, 23 minutes for groups of three)

(This test is also suitable for groups of three candidates; this only occurs as the last test of a session where a centre has an uneven number of candidates.)

There are two examiners. One (the Interlocutor) conducts the test, providing you with the necessary materials and explaining what you have to do. The other examiner (the Assessor) is introduced to you, but then takes no further part in the interaction.

Part 1 (3 minutes for pairs of candidates, 5 minutes for groups of three)

The Interlocutor first asks you and your partner a few questions. You are then asked to find out some information about each other, on topics such as hobbies, interests, future plans, etc. You are then asked further questions by the Interlocutor.

Part 2 (4 minutes for pairs of candidates, 6 minutes for groups of three)

You are each given the opportunity to talk for about a minute, and to comment briefly after your partner has spoken.

The Interlocutor gives you a set of pictures and asks you to talk about them for about one minute. The Interlocutor also asks you to let your partner(s) see your pictures.

Your partner / one of your partners is then given another set of pictures to look at and this candidate talks about these pictures for about one minute. The Interlocutor also asks this candidate to let their partner(s) see their pictures.

If a group of three candidates is being examined, the Interlocutor gives another set of pictures to the third candidate to look at. This candidate talks about these pictures for about a minute. The Interlocutor also asks this candidate to let their partners see their pictures.

When you have all had your turn, the Interlocutor asks you to look at each other's pictures again and answer together another question, which relates to all the pictures.

Part 3 (approximately 4 minutes for pairs of candidates, 6 minutes for groups of three)

In this part of the test you and your partner(s) are asked to talk together. The Interlocutor places a new set of pictures on the table in front of you. This stimulus provides the basis for a discussion. The Interlocutor then explains what you have to do.

Part 4 (approximately 4 minutes for pairs of candidates, 6 minutes for groups of three)

The Interlocutor asks some further questions, which leads to a more general discussion of what you have talked about in Part 3. You may comment on the answers of your partner(s) if you wish.

Test 3

PAPER 1   READING (1 hour 15 minutes)

Part 1

Answer questions **1–16** by referring to the magazine article about offices on page **57**. Indicate your answers **on the separate answer sheet**.

For questions **1–16**, choose your answers from the offices (**A–D**) described in the article. Some of the choices may be required more than once.

Of which office is the following stated?

Some of the staff like it and some don't.	1 ....
Advice from an expert has had a good effect.	2 ....
Staff there benefit from the range of work involved.	3 ....
Some members of staff prefer unsuitable furniture.	4 ....
A particular rule has been beneficial.	5 ....
The air quality is better than might be expected.	6 ....
It is often either very hot or very cold.	7 ....
Staff can work in privacy if they want to.	8 ....
The staff are not told what they can and cannot do there.	9 ....
There is not enough room for every member of staff to work.	10 ....
It would be better if the furniture were arranged differently.	11 ....
Evidence of the company's achievements is visible.	12 ....
Staff can control the temperature effectively.	13 ....
Staff appear to be under pressure.	14 ....
Working here is like being on display.	15 ....
The staff have made it a pleasant place to work in.	16 ....

IS YOUR OFFICE WORKING OK?

Fresh air and the right chairs are the key to a happy, healthy workforce, according to a new survey. We went to four contrasting offices, to find out how healthy and happy they were as working environments. On our expert panel were a building health consultant; an ergonomist, who studies people's working conditions; and an occupational psychologist. Here are their verdicts.

OFFICE A   ADVERTISING AGENCY

Building Health Consultant: This office is about as simple as it could possibly be; no central heating, no mechanical ventilation, windows opening straight onto the street. It is difficult to see why this space works but the occupants, who are part of a small, dynamic team, appear to have few complaints. They adapt to the changing seasons by opening doors and roof panels or switching on electric radiators – pretty much, perhaps, as they do in their own homes. This may be the key: a team of seven people have created a happy, homely working environment and do not have to put up with any externally imposed bureaucracy.

Ergonomist: The furniture here has evolved; no two pieces match. Much of it actually creates bad working postures. Chairs are old, most aren't adjustable and many are broken. Although in that way this environment is poor, the personnel have a varied work schedule, which they control – office work, out meeting clients, making presentations, and so on. This variety reduces the risk of fatigue, boredom or muscular problems.

Occupational Psychologist: Staff are delighted with the variety of work and the versatility of the office space. They said their office was 'just the right size' – small enough to know what colleagues were doing, large enough to be able to be on your own and focus on personal work. I found the office attractive and fun, simultaneously conveying images of efficiency and creativity.

OFFICE B   NEWS SERVICE

Building Health Consultant: While the office may not be very exciting, it appears comfortable and is not disliked by the staff. The air quality and general maintenance standards appear to be good. This is helped by a No Smoking policy.

Ergonomist: I was not surprised to learn that the company had already employed the services of an ergonomist. Chairs are excellent, lighting and computer equipment are good. Space provision is good, although the layout could be improved. But the environment is impersonal and unstimulating, with grey, bare walls.

Occupational Psychologist: Walls are bare apart from year planners and a poster describing maternity rights. Most staff have been there for at least five years and relationships are satisfactory. The office could be improved if desks were positioned to make the sharing of information easier. Proof of success or information on forthcoming projects could be displayed on the walls.

OFFICE C   BANK

Building Health Consultant: An office that produces mixed reactions from those working in it. The feeling inside is akin to being in a glass case, viewed by, and viewing, countless similar exhibits. Despite a mix of smokers and non-smokers in a relatively small space, the air did not appear to be stale. Even standing only 1.5 metres away from a smoker, it was not possible to smell his cigarette.

Ergonomist: The office area is, sadly, very standard and totally uninspiring. The desks are adequate, but only just. Not all the chairs being used for computer operation conform to requirements but this is user choice. Computer screens are often on small desk units with lowered keyboard shelves; this is no longer considered appropriate for modern equipment.

Occupational Psychologist: Staff are mutually supportive and well served by technology. Numerous communications awards are on display. The wood coloured panelling and brown carpet give a slightly sombre effect. The office is a buzz of activity.

OFFICE D   NEWSPAPER

Building Health Consultant: It is difficult to say anything good about this building. The air-conditioning control is very crude, resulting in large variations in temperature. The space is cluttered and most people have inadequate desk space. The office is very dusty – there are plenty of places for dust to lodge. The shed-type roof also collects dust, which, if disturbed, showers those sitting below.

Ergonomist: The furniture would be more at home in a carpentry workshop than in a high-tech industry. Most of the chairs are of little value to keyboard users, particularly those who are shorter than about 1.75 m. Many chairs are old, lack suitable adjustment and have armrests that prevent the user from getting sufficiently close to the desk.

Occupational Psychologist: Old brown chairs, soiled carpets, dust and dirt everywhere. A lot of scope for improvement – the place needs a good tidy-up, individual success could be more recognised, air conditioning needs to be improved immediately – there are so many smokers. Few conversations were going on when we visited; everybody seemed stressed and driven by deadlines. The company needs to adopt a policy of team-working.

Part 2

For questions **17–22**, you must choose which of the paragraphs **A–G** on page **59** fit into the numbered gaps in the following newspaper article. There is one extra paragraph, which does not fit in any of the gaps. Indicate your answers **on the separate answer sheet**.

Plugging in the home

Georgina McGuiness had taken a long career break from journalism and she felt out of touch with the changes brought about by technology. She recounts here how she was able to transform the family home into an efficient workplace.

The Christmas before last I turned 37 and realised that time was running out if I wanted to resurrect a career in journalism – which I believed had been washed down the plug-hole … the technological plug-hole.

A quick glance at my curriculum vitae showed that I was shamefully stuck in the 1980s, when a piece of carbon wedged in between several sheets of paper in a typewriter was the state of the art. It seemed that only a madman would let me loose on a computer in his newsroom. And why did most of the jobs advertised ask for experience in desktop publishing – which I didn't have?

| **17** | |

Clearly, there was a gaping hole in what was left of my career and I had to act quickly. Leaving home before the children did would be fraught with obstacles, or so I thought until I entered a competition in a local newspaper. Like a success story you read or hear about that only ever happens to other people, my family and I won a computer package.

| **18** | |

I had everything I would need for working from home – and I could still manage to take the children to school. They were confident with computers from the start, already well versed in them from school. I was much more hesitant, convinced that all my work would disappear without trace if I pressed the wrong button. I could not have been more wrong.

| **19** | |

I recently began freelancing for a magazine,

contributing about two articles a month, and I have become smug in the knowledge that I have the best of two worlds.

So how has the computer helped me? Since my schooldays I have always worked at a desk that can only be described as a chaotic mess.

| **20** | |

Spreadsheets help keep a record of income and expenses, and pre-formatted invoices and letterheads have saved me a lot of time and effort. For a journalist, getting on-line with the Internet means I can research stories, ask for further information on the bulletin board in the journalism or publishing forums and even discuss the pros and cons of working from home with people from all over the world.

| **21** | |

However, there is a growing band of people who have recently bought multi-media PCs, not just for the educational, leisure and entertainment facilities. In my street alone there appears to be a new type of technical cottage industry evolving from the sheer convenience of not having to join the commuter struggle into the city each day. So what characterises home workers as we move into the next century?

| **22** | |

Taking this into account, I seem to be well ahead of schedule. And who knows, one day I might be e-mailing a column to a newspaper in Melbourne or, better still, publishing my own magazine from home. It seems the sky, or should I say cyberspace, is the limit.

A Consequently, I was always losing scraps of paper containing vital bits of information. The computer has transformed me into an organised worker, particularly when it comes to office administration.

B If all this sounds too good to be true, there is a dark side to computing from home. You can be in isolation from physical human contact. There are the distractions of putting urgent jobs about the house first, and when the children are home there are power struggles in our house over whose turn it is to use the computer.

C To get an idea of the speed and convenience with which someone based at home can send their work back to the office, this article will be sent in a matter of minutes via a modem straight into the editor's computer.

D I thought I had a better chance of hosting a seminar in nuclear physics than attempting to lay out a page on a computer. I was the family technophobe; even pocket calculators were a mystery to me and I still don't know how to use the timer on the video.

E A report entitled *PC Usage in UK Homes* provides the following profile of the millennium computer user: 38 and well educated; 93% own a personal computer and 32% have a CD-ROM device; 38% have a laser printer and 50% a modem.

F Though far from being adroit, I did manage to learn the basic skills I needed – it was all so logical, easy and idiot-proof. And, like everything that you persevere with, you learn a little more each day.

G Supplied with a laptop computer to free my husband from his desk, and a personal computer for us all, we dived in at the deep end into a strange new world and terms such as *cyberspace, Internet* and *surfing* became commonplace in our vocabulary. We took to chatting like old pals via the Internet to strangers around the world. The children forsook the television and I set up a mini-office in a corner of the kitchen with a telephone-answering facility, a fax machine, a CD-ROM, and a modem linking me into the information superhighway.

Part 3

Read the following magazine article and answer questions **23–29** on page **61**. **On your answer sheet**, indicate the letter **A**, **B**, **C** or **D** against the number of each question. Give only one answer to each question.

Solar Survivor

Charles Clover ventures inside Britain's most environmentally-friendly home.

Southwell in Nottinghamshire is full of surprises. The first is Britain's least-known ancient cathedral, Southwell Minster, celebrated by writers of an environmental disposition for the pagan figures of 'green' men which medieval craftsmen carved into the decorations in its thirteenth-century chapter house. The second, appropriately enough, is Britain's greenest dwelling, the 'autonomous house', designed and built by Robert and Brenda Vale.

The Vales use rainwater for washing and drinking, recycle their sewage into garden compost and heat their house with waste heat from electrical appliances and their own body heat, together with that of their three teenage children and their two cats, Edison and Faraday. You could easily miss the traditional-looking house, roofed with clay pantiles, on a verdant corner plot 300 yards from the Minster. It was designed to echo the burnt-orange brick of the town's nineteenth-century buildings and won approval from the planners even though it is in a conservation area.

Ring the solar-powered doorbell and there is total silence. The house is super-insulated, with krypton-filled triple-glazed windows, which means that you do not hear a sound inside. Once inside and with your shoes off (at Robert's insistence), there is a monastic stillness. It is a sunny summer's day, the windows are closed and the conservatory is doing its normal job of warming the air before it ventilates the house. Vale apologises and moves through the house, opening ingenious ventilation shafts and windows. You need to create draughts because draught-proofing is everywhere: even Edison and Faraday have their own air-locked miniature door.

The Vales, who teach architecture at Nottingham University, were serious about the environment long before it hit the political agenda. They wrote a book on green architecture back in the 1970s, *The Autonomous House*. They began by designing a building which emitted no carbon dioxide. Then they got carried away and decided to do without mains water as well. They designed composting earth closets, lowered rainwater tanks into the cellar, and specified copper gutters to protect the drinking water, which they pass through two filters before use. Water from washing runs into the garden (the Vales don't have a dishwasher because they believe it is morally unacceptable to use strong detergents). Most details have a similar statement in mind.

'We wanted people to see that it was possible to design a house which would be far less detrimental to the environment, without having to live in the dark,' says Robert. 'It would not be medieval.' The house's only medieval aspect is aesthetic: the hall, which includes the hearth and the staircase, rises the full height of the building.

The Vales pay no water bills. And last winter the house used only nine units of electricity a day costing about 70p – which is roughly what other four bedroomed houses use on top of heating. Soon it will use even less, when £20,000 worth of solar water heating panels and generating equipment arrive and are erected in the garden. The house will draw electricity from the mains supply for cooking and running the appliances, but will generate a surplus of electricity. There will even be enough, one day, to charge an electric car. The only heating is a small wood-burning stove in the hall, which the Vales claim not to use except in the very coldest weather.

So is it warm in winter? One night in February when I happened to call on him, Robert was sitting reading. It was too warm to light the fire, he said. The room temperature on the first floor was 18°C, less than the generally expected temperature of living areas, but entirely comfortable, he claimed, because there are no draughts, no radiant heat loss, since everything you touch is at the same temperature. Perceived temperature depends on these factors. An Edwardian lady in the early years of the twentieth century was entirely comfortable at 12.5°C, he says, because of the insulation provided by her clothing. Those people who live in pre-1900 housing, he suggests, should simply go back to living as people did then. Somehow, it is difficult to think of this idea catching on.

The house's secret is that it is low-tech and there is little to go wrong. Almost everything was obtained from a builder's merchant and installed by local craftsmen. This made the house cheap to build – it cost the same price per square metre as low-cost housing for rent. Not surprisingly, the commercial building companies are determinedly resisting this idea.

23 According to the writer, the exterior of the Vales' house is

   A unique.
   B unattractive.
   C controversial.
   D unremarkable.

24 Why did Robert Vale apologise to the writer on his arrival?

   A The ventilation system had failed.
   B The temperature was uncomfortable.
   C The conservatory was not functioning properly.
   D The draughts were unwelcome.

25 What does the writer suggest about environmental issues in the fourth paragraph?

   A They have always been a difficult topic.
   B They have become a subject of political debate.
   C The Vales have changed their views in recent years.
   D The Vales have begun to take a political interest in the subject.

26 What does the writer imply about the decision not to use mains water in the Vales' house?

   A It was impractical.
   B It was later regretted.
   C It was an extreme choice.
   D It caused unexpected problems.

27 In Robert Vale's opinion, his home challenges the idea that houses designed with the environment in mind must be

   A draughty.
   B primitive.
   C small.
   D ugly.

28 The planned changes to the house's electrical system will mean that

   A the house will produce more electricity than it uses.
   B the Vales will not use electricity from the mains supply.
   C the house will use more electricity than it does now.
   D the Vales' electricity bills will remain at their current level.

29 According to Robert Vale, the house was comfortable in February because

   A no variations in temperature could be noticed.
   B 18°C was acceptable for ordinary houses.
   C it was not a particularly cold winter.
   D he had got used to the temperature.

Part 4

Answer questions **30–48** by referring to the magazine article on pages **63–64** about hotels and health farms. Indicate your answers **on the separate answer sheet**.

For questions **30–38**, answer by choosing from the list of places (**A–E**) on the right below. Some of the choices may be required more than once.
Note: When more than one answer is required, these may be given **in any order**.

Which section(s) of the article mention(s)		
a building specifically constructed for its present function?	30	**A Henlow Grange**
the cost of additional services?	31	**B Shrubland Hall**
the ease with which a range of treatments can be booked?	32	
the intention to expand the range of facilities?	33	**C Careys Manor**
the provision of outdoor activities?	34 .... 35	**D Cliveden**
the premises attracting different kinds of people?	36	
a particularly attractive setting for the buildings?	37 .... 38	**E Springs Hydro**

For questions **39–48**, answer by choosing from the list of journalists (**A–E**) on the right below. Some of the choices may be required more than once.
Note: When more than one answer is required, these may be given **in any order**.

Which journalist(s) state(s) that she/they		
felt that the assignment came at a good time for her?	39	**A Marcelle D'Argy Smith**
exercised to counter the effects of the food?	40 .... 41	**B Liz Gregory**
could not stay awake during a particular treatment?	42	
was amazed at the range of food?	43	**C Beverley D'Silva**
received attention for a physical complaint?	44 .... 45	**D Kay Letch**
was disconcerted by the term used to refer to the guests?	46	
did not view the quality of the food as an entirely good thing?	47	**E Eve Cameron**
felt unwell during her visit?	48	

RETREAT, RELAX, RECHARGE

Health farms and country house hotels offering spa facilities report that business is booming. We asked five journalists to check out some of the places that are available.

A   HENLOW GRANGE

I welcomed the opportunity to go to Henlow Grange for six days as I was tired and needed to relax. My room in the main part of the huge 18th-century house was the most comfortable possible and I was instantly soothed.

On Day One I did nothing and slept lots. But from Day Two I started going to body conditioning and doing as many classes as I could (stretch and tone, yoga, body alignment, to name but a few). All the instructors are highly trained. I couldn't believe how supple I began to feel as the week progressed.

They have every possible treatment, including aromatherapy (I've never been so relaxed), seaweed baths, manicures, and pedicures. The facial, which lasts for an hour, really does make you feel like a new person.

The staff in the treatment rooms deserve a bouquet. They couldn't have been friendlier, nicer or more professional. The whole atmosphere is one of vitality and enthusiasm. Henlow are planning a major refurbishment this year, which will include a half-size Olympic swimming pool and a Light Diet Room. Bicycles are available and you can ride around the grounds. If you're not feeling energetic and the weather's on your side, grab a magazine or enjoy a peaceful walk in the garden.

During my stay, my mood improved and so did my appetite. I left feeling wonderful and full of energy, which lasted for ages. I'm definitely due another visit. This is the *perfect* break for the stressed working woman. Save Room 5 for me!

Marcelle D'Argy Smith

B   SHRUBLAND HALL

The calm and relaxing atmosphere of this stately home was evident from the moment I climbed the vast staircase into the reception area. The Hall has an impressively decorated library, a charming conservatory and lots of space, so you don't have to speak to anyone if you don't want to.

On arrival everybody is given a medical, which includes an examination and a check on weight and blood pressure. We were all called patients, which I found a bit disquieting as I'm in good health. However, I was impressed that a shoulder problem discovered in the examination was immediately passed on to the fitness instructor and we worked on it in the group workshops and also in an extra session of individual instruction.

Each patient is given a specific diet to follow. Although I lost weight without fasting, I was still hungry enough to develop a fierce headache on the second day. A typical daily menu for me was a breakfast of grapefruit and honey, hot lemon and boiled water; a choice of salads for lunch; and a mixture of exotic fruit, yoghurt and a flask of hot broth for supper. If you're not fasting or on a light diet, then you'll eat in the main dining hall, where the food is tasty and nicely presented, so you needn't suffer too much! You have a massage or water therapy on alternate days. All extra treatments are competitively priced.

Liz Gregory

C   CAREYS MANOR

Careys is not a health farm and doesn't pretend to be. It's a fine old manor farm with inviting log fires and a spacious lounge. If you're counting calories, you'll have to miss out on the gourmet food. Rich sauces and delightful creamy confections are conjured up by the French chef. It's a good job the hotel has a fully-equipped gym and soft-water pool so I could work off some of the tempting indulgences. (You can opt for a 'health-conscious' diet if you really want to lose weight.) There is a spa bath, steam room, Swiss shower, sauna and treatment rooms. A big attraction is the sports injury clinic. I got an expert opinion on an old, sometimes painful, shoulder injury. The physiotherapist recommended good posture, remedial exercises and massage. Careys manages to be comfortable and luxurious, laid-back and sedate. If you want to break out, there is great surrounding countryside to explore.

Beverley D'Silva

D CLIVEDEN

Cliveden is a majestic country home and is also a five-star hotel that treats its guests like royalty. It offers health and beauty treatments, a well-equipped gym, saunas, swimming pool, tennis, horse riding, and much more. There are stunning woodland walks and gardens around the 376-acre National Trust estate.

And there's Waldo's, a highly-acclaimed restaurant with dishes to make you clutch your stomach. In ecstasy. It took me half an hour to read the dinner menu; the choice was staggering. The meal was wonderful, especially the sticky-toffee pudding with banana ice-cream. I climbed into bed a happy woman!

Next morning I dutifully spent a few hours in the gym playing with exercise equipment to burn off a few calories in time for my next meal. In the Pavilion I enjoyed a facial with gentle heat and essential oils. Then I had an aromatherapy massage.

I thought of all the other reports my fellow journalists would make, about fitness assessments, workouts, and beauty treatments to tone and firm the body. Cliveden has all these if you want to use them – before indulging yourself at Waldo's.

Kay Letch

E SPRINGS HYDRO

The best and the worst thing about Springs Hydro is the carrot cake. The best because it really is the most delicious I've ever tasted. The worst, because it's a huge slab of 360 calories, which sets you back if you want to lose weight. You have been warned! The second best thing is the fabulous aromatherapy massage. I chose the relaxing oils blend, dropped off to sleep twice during the massage, floated back to my room and had my most refreshing night's sleep in years.

The premises are modern and purpose-built, efficiently run, with up-to-the-minute facilities and luxurious bedrooms. There are plenty of therapists and beauty rooms so there's little difficulty in scheduling appointments. A variety of treatments are on offer, from manicures and pedicures to deep-cleansing facials and body treatments. The guests are an eclectic mix – from entire football teams to mums and daughters, best friends and singles. Ideally, I would have a break here about once a month.

Eve Cameron

PAPER 2   WRITING (2 hours)

Part 1

1 You are a member of the student committee at an international college. The Principal has recently decided to make changes to the college sports facilities and has asked the student committee to look at the plans and comment on them.

Read the Principal's memo below and look at the plans on page **66**. Read all the notes you have made of the student committee's comments on the memo and the plans, then **using the information appropriately**, write the letter to the Principal, commenting on the plans and offering the student committee's suggestions.

---

memo

To: **Student Committee**

From: **College Principal**

Re: **Proposed changes to Sports Centre**

I enclose a copy of the plan of the Sports Centre as it is now and a second plan showing the changes we intend to make. I am sure you will agree that the current problems will be (fully) resolved by the proposed changes.

don't agree

As I understand it, these problems are:
– indoor tennis court too busy
– gym under-used
– coffee bar too small
– sauna too far from pool.

To cover the costs of the changes I may have to introduce an entrance fee of (£5 per visit) unless you can suggest other ways of (funding) the changes.

open centre to public?

Please send me your comments as soon as possible. We do want to take account of students' views, as they are the ones who use the facilities.

no!

PLAN OF CURRENT SPORTS CENTRE

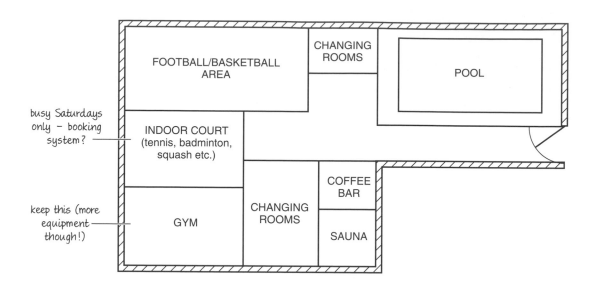

busy Saturdays only – booking system?

keep this (more equipment though!)

PRINCIPAL'S PLAN OF SPORTS CENTRE WITH PROPOSED CHANGES

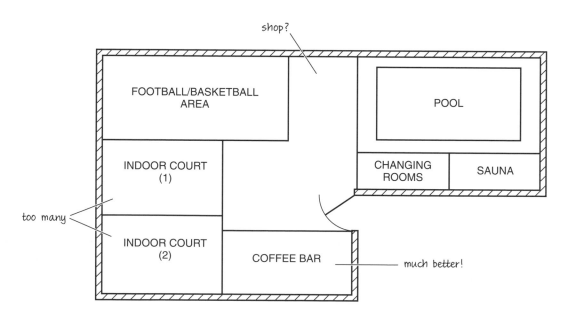

shop?

too many

much better!

Now write a **letter** to the Principal (approximately 250 words). You should use your own words as far as possible. You do not need to include postal addresses.

Part 2

Choose **one** of the following writing tasks. Your answer should follow exactly the instructions given. Write approximately 250 words.

2   You see the following announcement in a magazine called *Tourism Today*.

> Pop stars, sports personalities and film stars are often the most famous representatives of their countries. Who is the best known representative of your country? Write an article:
>
> ❱ telling us about this person
>
> ❱ explaining why he or she attracts so much interest
>
> ❱ giving your opinion about the image he or she presents.

Write your **article**.

3   You are a member of an English language social club. Some members of the club cannot attend an English course and would welcome suggestions and advice on how to improve their English independently. You have agreed to write a leaflet giving a number of ideas and practical tips for people learning without a teacher.

Write the **text for the leaflet**.

4   You have been asked to write a report for an international survey about attitudes to jobs in your country. You should:

- describe the ways in which some jobs have gained or lost respect during the past twenty years
- explain why you think this has occurred
- say what other changes in job status may take place in the future.

Write your **report**.

5   The company you work for is going to close some departments as the goods or services they provide are no longer required. Your department, however, is going to expand and will need some employees from the departments which are closing. As a result of this, your manager has asked you to write a proposal outlining the following:

- which staff should be re-trained
- what sort of re-training these members of staff will require
- how long the re-training will take
- how the company will benefit.

Write the **proposal**.

PAPER 3   ENGLISH IN USE (1 hour 30 minutes)

Part 1

For questions **1–15**, read the text below and then decide which word on page **69** best fits each space. Put the letter you choose for each question in the correct box on your answer sheet. The exercise begins with an example (**0**).

Example: | 0 | *B* | | 0 |

Holidays in South Carolina

Roaring across the bay in a motorised rubber boat, we were told by the captain to (**0**) ..... our eyes open. With the engine (**1**) ....., it wasn't long before half a dozen dolphins came swimming around us. Eventually, two came up (**2**) ..... beside the boat and popped their heads out of the water to give us a wide grin.

Dolphin watching is just one of the many unexpected attractions of a holiday in South Carolina, in the USA. The state has long been popular with golfers and, with dozens of (**3**) ..... in the area, it is (**4**) ..... a golfer's paradise. But even the keenest golfer needs other diversions and we soon found the resorts had plenty to (**5**) ....

In fact, Charleston, which is midway along the (**6**) ..... , is one of the most interesting cities in America and is where the first shots in the Civil War were (**7**) .... Taking a guided horse and carriage tour through the quiet back streets you get a real (**8**) ..... of the city's past. Strict regulations (**9**) ..... to buildings so that original (**10**) ..... are preserved.

South of Charleston lies Hilton Head, an island resort about 18 km long and (**11**) ..... like a foot. It has a fantastic sandy beach (**12**) ..... the length of the island and this is perfect for all manner of water sports. (**13**) ..... , if you feel like doing nothing, (**14**) ..... a chair and umbrella, head for an open (**15**) ..... and just sit back and watch the pelicans diving for fish.

0   A   stand   (B)   keep   C   hold   D   fix

1   A   turned out   B   turned away   C   turned off   D   turned over

2   A   direct   B   right   C   precise   D   exact

3   A   courses   B   pitches   C   grounds   D   courts

4   A   fully   B   truly   C   honestly   D   purely

5   A   show   B   provide   C   offer   D   supply

6   A   beach   B   coast   C   sea   D   shore

7   A   thrown   B   aimed   C   pulled   D   fired

8   A   significance   B   meaning   C   sense   D   comprehension

9   A   apply   B   happen   C   agree   D   occur

10 A   points   B   characters   C   aspects   D   features

11 A   formed   B   shaped   C   made   D   moulded

12 A   lying   B   running   C   going   D   following

13 A   Alternately   B   Conversely   C   Contrastingly   D   Alternatively

14 A   charge   B   lend   C   hire   D   loan

15 A   space   B   room   C   gap   D   place

Part 2

For questions **16–30**, complete the following article by writing each missing word in the correct box on your answer sheet. **Use only one word for each space**. The exercise begins with an example (**0**).

Example:

0	*most*	0

The Sahara Marathon

One of the (**0**) ..... amazing marathon races in the world is the Marathon of the Sands. It takes place every April in the Sahara Desert in the south of Morocco, a part of the world (**16**) ..... temperatures can reach forty degrees centigrade. The standard length of a marathon is 42.5 kilometres but (**17**) ..... one is 230 kilometres long and takes seven days to complete. It began in 1986 and now attracts about two hundred runners, the majority of (**18**) ..... ages range from seventeen to forty-seven. About half of (**19**) ..... come from France and the rest from all over the world. From Britain it costs £1,750 to enter, (**20**) ..... includes return air fares. The race is rapidly (**21**) ..... more and more popular (**22**) ....., or perhaps because of, the harsh conditions that runners must endure. They have to carry food and (**23**) ..... else they need (**24**) ..... seven days in a rucksack weighing no more than twelve kilograms. In (**25**) ..... to this, they are given a litre and a half of water every ten kilometres. Incredibly, nearly (**26**) ..... the runners finish the course. (**27**) ..... man, Ibrahim El Joual, has taken part in every race since 1986. Runners do suffer terrible physical hardships. Sometimes they lose toenails and skin peels (**28**) ..... their feet. However, doctors are always on hand to deal (**29**) ..... minor injuries and to make sure that runners do not push (**30**) ..... too far.

Part 3

In **most** lines of the following text, there is **either** a spelling **or** a punctuation error. For each numbered line **31–46**, write the correctly spelt word or show the correct punctuation in the box on your answer sheet. **Some lines are correct**. Indicate these lines with a tick (✔) in the box. The exercise begins with three examples (**0**), (**00**) and (**000**).

Examples:	0	✔	0
	00	*name, was*	00
	000	*immigrant*	000

Food Fame

0   Henry John Heinz, the founder of the gigantic food processing and

00   canning empire that bears his name was born in 1844 in Pittsburgh,

000 Pennsylvania, of German imigrant parents. When he was 25, he

31   formed a partnership with an old family freind, Larry Noble, selling

32   horseradish sauce in clear glass jars (previously, green glass had

33   disgiused the dishonest practice of substituting the horseradish with

34   other vegetables). So began the Heinz and Noble reputation for quality

35   and honesty. There products were also sold with the promise that they

36   did not contain artificial flavours and colours, long before such facters

37   were thought desirable Heinz & Noble steadily added other lines,

38   including pickles, and in 1876, Heinz formed an other company with

39   his brother and a cousin. One of the first products made was ketchup

40   a food found in every American household. This had previously been

41   made on a domestic scale and involved the whole family stirring a hugh

42   pot over an enormous open fire for an entire day. The bussiness was

43   sufficiently successful by 1886 for the Heinz family to visit Europe.

44   The company sold it's first products in Britain to an exclusive London

45   store, astonishing them by daring to enter throughth the front door,

46   rather than the tradesmens entrance, as was expected at that time.

Part 4

For questions **47–61**, read the two texts on pages **72** and **73**. Use the words in the boxes to the right of the texts to form **one** word that fits in the same numbered space in the text. Write the new word in the correct box on your answer sheet. The exercise begins with an example (**0**).

Example: | **0** | *stardom* | **0** |
| --- | --- | --- |

EXTRACT FROM A MAGAZINE ARTICLE

Want to be a Star?

Lots of us dream of being famous. For some, it's a desire for
(0) ..... in the movies, the theatre or on TV. For others, it's the
(47) ..... appeal of music, whether it's classical or rock. But the
reality is that getting to the top in any of the performing arts is
(48) ..... hard work.

    For every actor who makes it, there are thousands of (49) .....
youngsters working as waiters. For every top band, there are
(50) ..... others eager to play anywhere. Many of them have
(51) ..... but this alone may be (52) ..... . For some it's a good
idea to take a course to learn more of the (53) ..... so that this
talent can be developed.

(0)	STAR
(47)	UNIVERSE
(48)	AMAZE
(49)	HOPE
(50)	COUNT
(51)	ABLE
(52)	SUFFICIENT
(53)	BASE

JOB ADVERTISEMENT

President, International Institute for Energy Conservation

The International Institute for Energy Conservation is a non profit making **(54)** ..... working in developing countries. The thirty-person staff is based in Washington DC with four international offices. Applications are invited for the full-time position of President. The successful **(55)** ..... will have a proven record of **(56)** ..... in fund-raising, excellent **(57)** ..... skills and will have demonstrated **(58)** ..... skills through the practical implementation of projects. The President is required to travel **(59)** ..... and should have experience of working in multicultural environments. A minimum requirement is **(60)** ..... practical experience in energy **(61)** ..... programmes as well as a demonstrable knowledge of this field.

Applications or nominations should be sent to:
Charles Palmer, 899 University Avenue, Toronto, Canada.

(54)	FOUND
(55)	APPLY
(56)	EFFECT
(57)	MANAGE
(58)	LEAD
(59)	EXTEND
(60)	SUBSTANCE
(61)	EFFICIENT

Part 5

For questions **62–74**, read the following leaflet and use the information in it to complete the numbered gaps in the letter on page **75**. The words you need **do not** occur in the leaflet. **Use no more than two words for each gap**. The exercise begins with an example (**0**).

Example: | **0** | *staying there* | | **0** |

HOTEL INFORMATION LEAFLET

> **HOTEL SERVICES**
>
> - Car parking is available for residents but the hotel will not be liable in respect of loss or damage to any vehicle. Car keys should be deposited at Reception for safekeeping.
>
> - Messages will be delivered to your room, or in your absence, kept at Reception until your return. All incoming post will be handled in the same way.
>
> - Facsimile messages may be sent via Reception. The cost of these will be added to your bill.
>
> - Light refreshments can be ordered through the 24-hour Room Service.
>
> - If you wish to make use of the laundry service, please deposit items in the bag provided in your room and they will be returned the following day.
>
> - Guests are reminded to vacate their rooms by 11 am on the day of their departure. Should you require assistance with your luggage, please dial '0' for a porter, who can also arrange storage if necessary.
>
> - If you wish to settle the bill by personal cheque, it must be supported by a cheque guarantee card.
>
> - Invoices can only be sent to companies if an agreement has been made in writing a minimum of seven days prior to arrival.

LETTER

Dear Julie

Thanks for your letter. You wanted to know about the hotel I stayed in when I was in London last month.

Anyone **(0)** ..... can park in the hotel car park. However, the hotel won't accept **(62)** ..... if anything happens to your car. It's best to **(63)** ..... your keys in Reception. They are very organised – the Reception Staff will take messages that come for you if you're **(64)** ..... . It's the same for **(65)** ..... which arrive for you. You can send faxes, but that service is **(66)** ..... . If you get **(67)** ..... at any time, you can ring Room Service. If you want any of your **(68)** ..... put them into the laundry bag in your room and you'll **(69)** ..... back the following day.

You have to get out of your room by 11 am on the day that **(70)** ..... . You can ring the porter if you want help with your **(71)** ..... and he can also arrange storage for them.

Remember, they won't take cheques **(72)** ..... have a cheque guarantee card. If your company's **(73)** ..... , make sure they write and arrange it at least **(74)** ..... before you arrive.

I hope everything goes well.

With best wishes

Jane

Part 6

For questions **75–80**, read the following text and then choose from the list **A–J** given below the best phrase to fill each of the spaces. Write one letter (**A–J**) in the correct box on your answer sheet. Each correct phrase may only be used once. **Some of the suggested answers do not fit at all.** The exercise begins with an example (**0**).

Example:

Interviews

Many people are unsure of how to behave in interviews. Often, the temptation is to present yourself not as you really are, but as what you think the interviewer is looking for. We have all heard of people who got their big breaks by saying they knew exactly what to do **(0)** ..... . However, it seems that most Careers Advisers would recommend a more honest approach. You may find yourself exaggerating a little, but the trick is not **(75)** ..... .

When questioned about the qualities they were looking for in people applying for jobs, most interviewers saw fitting into the corporate culture and a willingness **(76)** ..... as very important. In the interview, however, it is this skill of relating to other people that is so difficult **(77)** ..... ; critics argue that, as a result, interviewers often show the tendency **(78)** ..... .

When getting ready for an interview, preparing answers is an obvious tactic, but you should always pay extremely careful attention to what is asked. It is all too easy **(79)** ..... . Always try to extend your answers beyond a brief yes or no, but don't go on for ever. If you need to clarify what the interviewer means, ask a question of your own, taking care not **(80)** ..... . Remember your future may be in his or her hands.

A to select people most like themselves
B to underestimate your own ability
C to keep to the point
D to overdo it
E to judge accurately
F to imply that the interviewer is at fault
G to misinterpret a question
H to do a job when they didn't
I to work as part of a team

J to please the interviewer

Visual materials for the Speaking test

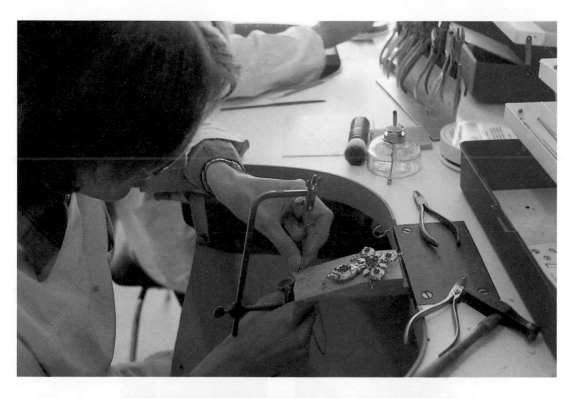

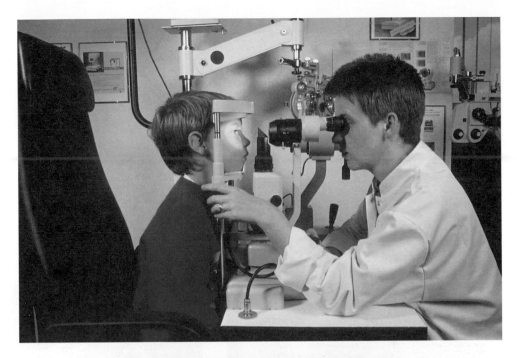

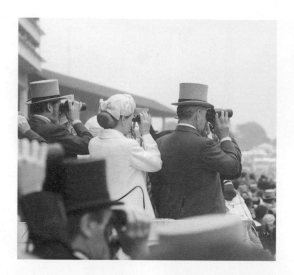

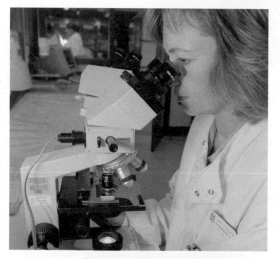

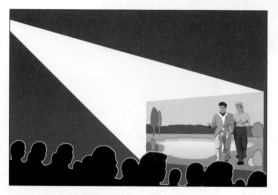

12A

13

12B

PAPER 4   LISTENING (approximately 45 minutes)

Part 1

You will hear someone giving a radio talk about postage stamps. For questions **1–8**, complete the sentences.

You will hear the recording twice.

POSTAGE STAMPS

It would be wrong to think that stamps are [_____ 1]

Stamps must stay on letters when machines move them at

[_____ 2]

The inks must not [_____ 3] people when handled.

The paper used for stamps feels [_____ 4]

It is important that sheets of stamps [_____ 5]

The acidity of the paper used must be [_____ 6]

The Post Office produces [_____ 7]

of special stamps for collectors.

The Post Office tries to avoid producing stamps which have quality or colour

[_____ 8]

Part 2

You will hear an introduction to a radio phone-in programme about modern lifestyles. For questions **9–15**, complete the sentences.

- **Listen very carefully as you will hear the recording ONCE only.**

MODERN LIFESTYLES

In Australia, Ron Clarke worked as an [_____ **9**]

He manages a number of [_____ **10**]

He calls his approach to life [_____ **11**]

He has just finished [_____ **12**]

He thinks you can improve your lifestyle by making time for

[_____ **13**]

Ron thinks it is a good idea to go out in the [_____ **14**]

He also thinks it is a bad idea to go on [_____ **15**]

Part 3

You will hear an interview with an engineer called Roger Moffat, whose working life has changed dramatically over the last ten years. For questions **16–22**, choose the correct answer **A**, **B**, **C** or **D**.

You will hear the recording twice.

16 The interviewer says that Roger is the kind of person who

   A is reluctant to try something different.
   B does not want to spend his money.
   C enjoys entertaining others.
   D is happy to reveal the tricks of his trade.

17 How did Roger feel initially about what happened ten years ago?

   A angry
   B resigned
   C depressed
   D disinterested

18 Roger regards his early days in business as

   A frustrating.
   B demanding.
   C irrelevant.
   D boring.

19 What does Roger feel is the greatest benefit of running his own business?

   A He arranges his free time as he pleases.
   B He gets on better with other people.
   C He has more leisure time than before.
   D He is free of an environment he disliked.

20 What is Roger's attitude towards his future?

   A He considers his position to be no less secure than before.
   B He thinks he'll be more vulnerable than he used to be.
   C He'd feel financially more secure working for someone else.
   D He considers himself too old to change direction again.

21 Which description best sums up Roger's appraisal of engineers?

   A dedicated workers
   B creative artists
   C well-balanced realists
   D powerful leaders

22 What does Roger find most satisfying about the 'tools of his trade'?

   A They are intricate beyond belief.
   B They are the creations of colleagues.
   C They are theoretical in design.
   D They are exciting to contemplate.

Part 4

You will hear five short extracts in which different people give their views on what they like to read when they go on holiday. Each extract has two questions. For questions **23–32**, choose the correct answer **A**, **B** or **C**.

You will hear the recording **twice**.

Speaker 1

23 The first speaker now reads books which

   A may impress other people.
   B help pass the time.
   C remind him of his country.

24 He thinks that holiday reading should be

   A serious and short.
   B easy to read.
   C long and absorbing.

Speaker 2

25 The second speaker reads books which

   A make him think of home.
   B help him relax.
   C offer an alternative to everyday life.

26 In airports, this speaker finds

   A it's difficult to concentrate.
   B you can't buy anything worth reading.
   C it's good to have a book if you're delayed.

Speaker 3

27 The third speaker reads books which

   A help learn a foreign language.
   B remind her of home.
   C inform her about places she visits.

28 She finds that

   A books can be comforting.
   B the journey home is always harder.
   C books can help you make friends.

Speaker 4

29 The fourth speaker reads books which

   A remind him of people he's met.
   B make a change from his work.
   C are set somewhere he doesn't know.

30 His work involves

   A a lot of travel.
   B studying classical literature.
   C looking out for new words.

Speaker 5

31 The fifth speaker reads books which

   A offer an escape from everyday life.
   B surprise other people.
   C are set somewhere she doesn't know.

32 She thinks a book can

   A be better than a holiday.
   B be a substitute for a holiday.
   C make a big difference to a holiday.

PAPER 5   SPEAKING (15 minutes)

There are two examiners. One (the Interlocutor) conducts the test, providing you with the necessary materials and explaining what you have to do. The other examiner (the Assessor) is introduced to you, but then takes no further part in the interaction.

Part 1 (3 minutes)

The Interlocutor first asks you and your partner a few questions. You are then asked to find out some information about each other, on topics such as hobbies, interests, future plans, etc. You are then asked further questions by the Interlocutor.

Part 2 (4 minutes)

You are each given the opportunity to talk for about a minute, and to comment briefly after your partner has spoken.

   The Interlocutor gives you a set of pictures and asks you to talk about them for about one minute. It is important to listen carefully to the Interlocutor's instructions. The Interlocutor then asks your partner a question about your pictures and your partner responds briefly.

   You are then given another set of pictures to look at. Your partner talks about these pictures for about one minute. This time the Interlocutor asks you a question about your partner's pictures and you respond briefly.

Part 3 (approximately 4 minutes)

In this part of the test you and your partner are asked to talk together. The Interlocutor places a new set of pictures on the table between you. This stimulus provides the basis for a discussion. The Interlocutor explains what you have to do.

Part 4 (approximately 4 minutes)

The Interlocutor asks some further questions, which leads to a more general discussion of what you have talked about in Part 3. You may comment on your partner's answers if you wish.

Test 4

PAPER 1   READING (1 hour 15 minutes)

Part 1

Answer questions **1–15** by referring to the magazine article on page **83** about leadership at work. Indicate your answers **on the separate answer sheet**.

For questions **1–15**, answer by choosing from the sections of the article (**A–F**) on page **83**. Some of the choices may be required more than once.

In which section of the article are the following mentioned?

deciding to let other people take charge	1 ....
sounding as if you mean what you say	2 ....
not feeling valued in your place of work	3 ....
knowing when it is best not to consult others	4 ....
having the same positive feelings as others	5 ....
considering your professional future	6 ....
wanting to work within certain limits	7 ....
being unaware of your capabilities	8 ....
being prepared to be unpopular	9 ....
realising how leadership may apply to your situation	10 ....
being unfairly blamed	11 ....
being forced to make a big effort	12 ....
being able to turn failure into success	13 ....
achieving more than you set out to do	14 ....
paying attention to other people's opinions	15 ....

CAREER POWER

Get the leading edge – motivate yourself to take full control at work.

A   What makes a good leader? A leader is one who inspires, an agent of change, a developer who shows the way forward. Leadership is not about breeding or height – taller being better, as the early theorists believed. It's not simply about intelligence, either. Pat Dixon, author of the book *Making the Difference: Women and Men in the Workplace*, says that leadership is about 'making things happen through people who are as enthusiastic and interested as you are'.

Enthusiasm is a key element and, to convey it and encourage it in others, a good leader should be able to speak out articulately and with conviction. 'It's having the confidence to say "I *believe*" instead of "I think",' maintains Dixon.

B   John van Maurik, director of a *Leadership in Management* course, says, 'Most people have a far greater potential for leadership than they realise. The process of becoming a leader is recognising those latent talents, developing them and using them.'

In one sense, we are all born leaders – we just need the right circumstances in which to flourish. While it's quite easy to recognise leadership in the grand sense – be it in the form of figures like Emmeline Pankhurst, Mahatma Ghandi or even Richard Branson – it may be more difficult to relate it to our own workplace. And yet this quality is now regarded as the cornerstone of effective management.

C   Consider the best and worst boss you've ever had. They may have been equally good at setting objectives, meeting deadlines and budgets. But what about how they achieved them? The best leader will have motivated you, and may have driven you hard. But he would have also given you support. The worst leader would have made you feel like a small cog in the corporate machinery and kept information from you, and then when things went wrong would have reacted as if it were your fault. The first led (very well); the second simply managed (very badly).

D   Leaders and managers can be seen as different animals. Managers tend to enjoy working according to set boundaries. Leaders create their own horizons. 'A good manager can keep even an inefficient company running relatively smoothly,' writes Micheal Shea, the author of *Leadership Rules*. 'But a good leader can transform a demoralised organisation – whether it's a company, a football team or a nation.'

E   Whether you're the boss or a middle manager, you can benefit from improving your leadership skills. There are definite lessons to be learnt:
- Leadership is something we do best when we *choose* to do it. So find out where your passions and convictions lie. Next time you feel inspired to lead, harness the energy it gives you and act on it.
- Start *thinking* of yourself as a leader. Your ability to lead is a powerful part of you. Recognise it.
- Collaboration can be fine, but there will be times when firm leadership is required. Experiment with your style. If you are a natural transactor, try being the negotiator. If you always ask for the views of others, try taking the lead. Watch how the outcome is changed by this change in you.
- You have to set goals, then beat them. Look at the demands of your job and define those where being a leader will greatly enhance your effectiveness and career prospects.

F
- Leadership does not simply happen. It can only develop from actually taking the lead, from taking risks and learning from mistakes. Learn how to delegate and motivate; organise and chastise; praise and raise.
- Don't assume that your way of leading will immediately win over colleagues. It may even alienate them. Keep working on your communication skills. *You* don't have to be liked – but your ideas and accomplishments *do*.
- Be visible and accessible to those who are important. But bear in mind that it can lend mystique to maintain a distance.
- You don't have to lead all the time. Be clear on where your contribution is vital and how you can help others to develop as leaders.

Part 2

For questions **16–22**, choose which of the paragraphs **A–H** on page **85** fit into the numbered gaps in the following newspaper article. There is one extra paragraph, which does not fit in any of the gaps. Indicate your answers **on the separate answer sheet**.

SCIENCE FLYING IN THE FACE OF GRAVITY

Journalist Tom Mumford joins students using weightlessness to test their theories.

It looked like just another aircraft from the outside. The pilot told his young passengers that it was built in 1964, a Boeing KC-135 refuelling tanker, based on the Boeing 707 passenger craft.

16

There were almost no windows, but it was eerily illuminated by lights along the padded walls. Most of the seats had been ripped out, apart from a few at the back, where the pale-faced, budding scientists took their places with the air of condemned men.

17

Those with the best ideas won a place on this unusual flight, which is best described as the most extraordinary roller-coaster ride yet devised. For the next two hours the Boeing's flight would resemble that of an enormous bird which had lost its reason, shooting upwards towards the heavens before hurtling towards Earth.

18

In the few silent seconds between ascending and falling, the aircraft and everything inside it become weightless, and the 13 students would, in theory, feel themselves closer to the moon than the Earth. The aircraft took off smoothly enough, but any lingering illusions the young scientists and I had that we were on anything like a scheduled passenger service were quickly dispelled when the pilot put the Boeing into a 45-degree climb which lasted around 20 seconds. The engines strained wildly, blood drained from our heads, and bodies were scattered across the cabin floor.

19

We floated aimlessly; the idea of going anywhere was itself confusing. Left or right, up or down, no longer had any meaning. Only gravity, by rooting us somewhere, permits us to appreciate the possibility of going somewhere else.

20

Our first curve completed, there were those who turned green at the thought of the 29 to follow. Thirty curves added up to ten minutes 'space time' for experiments and the Dutch students were soon studying the movements of Leonardo, their robotic cat, hoping to discover how it is that cats always land on their feet.

21

Next to the slightly stunned acrobatic robocat, a German team from the University of Aachen investigated how the quality of joins in metal is affected by the absence of gravity, with an eye to the construction of tomorrow's space stations.

Another team of students, from Utah State University, examined the possibility of creating solar sails from thin liquid films hardened in ultra-violet sunlight. Their flight was spent attempting to produce the films under microgravity. They believe that once the process is perfected, satellites could be equipped with solar sails that use the sun's radiation just as a yacht's sails use the wind.

22

This was a feeling that would stay with us for a long time. 'It was an unforgettable experience,' said one of the students. 'I was already aiming to become an astronaut, but now I want to even more.'

A The intention was to achieve a kind of state of grace at the top of each curve. As the pilot cuts the engines at 3,000 metres, the aircraft throws itself still higher by virtue of its own momentum before gravity takes over and it plummets earthwards again.

B After two hours spent swinging between heaven and Earth, that morning's breakfast felt unstable, but the predominant sensation was exhilaration, not nausea.

C After ten seconds of freefall descent, the pilot pulled the aircraft out of its nose dive. The return of gravity was less immediate than its loss, but was still sudden enough to ensure that some of the students came down with a bump.

D At the appropriate moment the device they had built to investigate this was released, floating belly-up, and one of the students succeeded in turning it belly-down with radio-controlled movements. The next curve was nearly its last, however, when another student landed on top of it during a less well managed return to gravitational pull.

E For 12 months, they had competed with other students from across the continent to participate in the flight. The challenge, offered by the European Space Agency, had been to suggest imaginative experiments to be conducted in weightless conditions.

F It was at that point that the jury of scientists were faced with the task of selecting from these experiments. They were obviously pleased by the quality: 'We need new ideas and new people like this in the space sciences,' a spokesman said.

G Then the engines cut out and the transition to weightlessness was nearly instantaneous. For 20 seconds we conducted a ghostly dance in the unreal silence: the floor had become a vast trampoline, and one footstep was enough to launch us headlong towards the ceiling.

H But appearances were deceptive, and the 13 students from Europe and America who boarded were in for the flight of their lives. Inside, it had become a long white tunnel.

Part 3

Read the following newspaper article about a 'mystery visitor' who inspects hotels for a guide book, and answer questions **23–29** on page **87**. **On your answer sheet**, indicate the letter **A**, **B**, **C** or **D** against the number of each question. Give only one answer to each question.

The Hotel Inspector

Sue Brown judges hotels for a living.
Christopher Middleton watched her in action.

One minute into the annual inspection and things are already going wrong for the Globe Hotel. Not that they know it yet. The receptionist reciting room rates over the phone to a potential guest is still blissfully unaware of the identity of the real guest she is doggedly ignoring. 'Hasn't even acknowledged us,' Sue Brown says out of the corner of her mouth. 'Very poor.' It is a classic arrival-phase error, and one that Sue has encountered scores of times in her 11 years as an inspector. 'But this isn't an ordinary three-star place,' she protests. 'It has three *red* stars, and I would expect better.'

To be the possessor of red stars means that the Globe is rated among the top 130 of the 4,000 listed in the hotel guide published by the organisation she works for. However, even before our frosty welcome, a chill has entered the air. Access from the car park has been via an unmanned door, operated by an impersonal buzzer, followed by a long, twisting, deserted corridor leading to the hotel entrance. 'Again, not what I had expected,' says Sue.

Could things get worse? They could. 'We seem to have no record of your booking,' announces the receptionist, in her best sing-song *how-may-I-help-you* voice.

It turns out that a dozen of the hotel's 15 rooms are unoccupied that night. One is on the top floor. It is not to the inspector's taste: stuffiness is one criticism, the other is a gaping panel at the back of the wardrobe, behind which is a large hole in the wall.

When she began her inspecting career, she earned an early reputation for toughness. '*The Woman in Black*, I was known as,' she recalls, 'which was funny, because I never used to wear black. And I've never been too tough.' Not that you would know it the next morning when, after paying her bill, she suddenly reveals her identity to the Globe's general manager, Robin Greaves. From the look on his face, her arrival has caused terror.

Even before she says anything else, he expresses abject apologies for the unpleasant smell in the main lounge. 'We think there's a blocked drain there,' he sighs. 'The whole floor will probably have to come up.' Sue gently suggests that as well as sorting out the plumbing, he might also prevail upon his staff not to usher guests into the room so readily. 'Best, perhaps, to steer them to the other lounge,' she says. Greaves nods with glum enthusiasm and gamely takes notes. He has been at the Globe for only five months, and you can see him struggling to believe Sue when she says that this dissection of the hotel can only be for the good of the place in the long run.

Not that it's all on the negative side. Singled out for commendation are Emma, the assistant manager, and Trudy, the young waitress, who dished out a sheaf of notes about the building's 400-year history. Dinner, too, has done enough to maintain the hotel's two-rosette food rating, thereby encouraging Greaves to push his luck a bit. 'So what do we have to do to get three rosettes?' he enquires. Sue's suggestions include: '*Not serve a pudding that collapses.*' The brief flicker of light in Greaves' eyes goes out.

It is Sue Brown's unenviable job to voice the complaints the rest of us more cowardly consumers do not have the courage to articulate. 'Sometimes one can be treading on very delicate ground. I remember, in one case, a woman rang to complain I'd got her son the sack. All I could say was the truth, which was that he'd served me apple pie with his fingers.' Comeback letters involve spurious allegations of everything, from a superior attitude to demanding bribes. 'You come to expect it after a while, but it hurts every time,' she says.

Sue is required not just to relate her findings to the hotelier verbally, but also to send them a full written report. They are, after all, paying for the privilege of her putting them straight. (There is an annual fee for inclusion in the guide.) Nevertheless, being singled out for red-star treatment makes it more than worthwhile. So it is reassuring for Greaves to hear that Sue is not going to recommend that the Globe be stripped of its red stars. That is the good news. The bad is that another inspector will be back in the course of the next two months to make sure that everything has been put right. 'Good,' smiles Greaves unconvincingly. 'We'll look forward to that.'

23   When Sue Brown arrived at the hotel reception desk,

    A   the receptionist pretended not to notice she was there.
    B   she was not surprised by what happened there.
    C   she decided not to form any judgements immediately.
    D   the receptionist was being impolite on the phone.

24   On her arrival at the hotel, Sue was dissatisfied with

    A   the temperature in the hotel.
    B   the sound of the receptionist's voice.
    C   the position of the room she was given.
    D   the distance from the car park to the hotel.

25   What does the writer say about Sue's reputation?

    A   It has changed.
    B   It frightens people.
    C   It is thoroughly undeserved.
    D   It causes Sue considerable concern.

26   When talking about the problem in the main lounge, Robin Greaves

    A   assumes that Sue is unaware of it.
    B   blames the problem on other people.
    C   doubts that Sue's comments will be of benefit to the hotel.
    D   agrees that his lack of experience has contributed to the problem.

27   When Sue makes positive comments about the hotel, Robin Greaves

    A   agrees with her views on certain members of his staff.
    B   becomes hopeful that she will increase its food rating.
    C   finds it impossible to believe that she means them.
    D   reminds her that they outweigh her criticisms of it.

28   Angry reactions to Sue's comments on hotels

    A   are something she always finds upsetting.
    B   sometimes make her regret what she has said.
    C   are often caused by the fact that hotels have to pay for them.
    D   sometimes indicate that people have not really understood them.

29   When Sue leaves the hotel, Robin Greaves

    A   is confident that the next inspection will be better.
    B   feels he has succeeded in giving her a good impression.
    C   decides to ignore what she has told him about the hotel.
    D   tries to look pleased that there will be another inspection.

Part 4

Answer questions **30–47** by referring to the magazine article about mountain climbing on pages **89–90**. Indicate your answers **on the separate answer sheet**.

For questions **30–47**, answer by choosing from the sections of the article (**A–G**) on pages **89–90**. Some of the choices may be required more than once.

Note: When more than one answer is required, these may be given **in any order**.

In which section or sections are the following mentioned?

the established route up the mountain being crowded	**30** ....
the primary concern being to complete the climb without injury	**31** ....
cautionary advice being given about particular dangers	**32** ....
the uplifting nature of the place	**33** ....
the climbers being unable to find their way at the base of the mountain	**34** ....
the writer joining a colleague's group of climbers	**35** ....
a particular mountaineering technique being pioneered on a new route	**36** ....
reaching the summit more quickly than anticipated	**37** ....
a sudden decision to take a different route	**38** .... **39** ....
the irrational behaviour of the writer's colleague	**40** ....
the ill effects of climbing at height being greater in that particular area	**41** ....
the complete silence of the area	**42** ....
the mistaken assumption that they had reached the top	**43** ....
the writer beginning to consider climbing all seven mountains	**44** ....
the journey to the region having a dual purpose	**45** ....
the disappointment felt at being unable to see the view from the mountain top	**46** ....
an attempt to make a charge for entering the area	**47** ....

Seven Up

Mountaineer Doug Scott shares with his readers the mystical experience of conquering the highest peak on each continent: the Seven Summits.

My quest to climb the Seven Summits came late in life. I will take them in the order of my climbing them.

A Mt. Everest, Asia (8,848m)

We were in a snow cave 91m below the summit when my climbing partner, Dougal Haston, began a conversation with Dave Clark, our Equipment Officer, about the relative merits of various sleeping bags. I thought this was strange, as only Dougal and I were present. Putting this down to oxygen deprivation, I then found myself talking to my feet. Already the cold was getting into the balls of my feet and I recalled other climbers who had lost fingers and toes from frostbite. It wasn't survival that was worrying us so much as the *quality* of our survival.

Over the next two days I relived our time spent on the summit ridge. I realised that I couldn't have been there with a better man than Dougal Haston. He inspired great confidence in me and by now I was climbing with a calm presentiment that somehow or other it was all going to work out. I realised I had to get a better rhythm going in order to reach the summit – which is what I did.

B Mt. McKinley, North America (6,194m)

This mountain is regarded as the most treacherous in the world. In April 1976 Dougal and I arrived at the Kahiltna Glacier and spent four days humping equipment and food up to the base. Only after the first day of climbing did we realise the enormity of our undertaking. On the lower face we followed a route put up in 1967, but at half height we pursued a new route, as planned, heading directly for the upper snow basin and the summit. We decided to climb 'alpine style', with our equipment and food on our backs. It would be the first time a major new route had been climbed here in such a way.

We climbed up the compressed snow of an avalanche scar to camp under a rocky cliff and by the third day my sleeping bag was sodden. We spent the third night on a windswept ridge; by now we were both suffering. Mt. McKinley, because the air pressure in the polar regions is lower, has an impact on the body out of all proportion to its altitude. It seemed to us that we were up at around 7,000m, instead of 6,100m. We packed our bags and finally staggered onto the summit and down the other side, triumphant.

C Kilimanjaro, Africa (5,895m)

In September 1976, Paul Braithwaite and I flew to Nairobi with the intention of climbing Mt. Kenya. It was through the unexpected offer of a free ride to the Tanzanian side of Kilimanjaro that we came to climb Africa's highest mountain.

On our approach we got ourselves lost in the dense jungles of the lower slopes. Our situation became serious because water is scarce. On the second day we came across luminous arrows painted on trees and a trail of rubbish which brought us to a rock pool. Never before had I been so pleased to find rubbish on a mountain.

We attempted a direct start to the breach wall, which is a 305m-high icicle. After a deluge of falling rock and ice we prudently retired and opted instead for the Umbwe route to gain the surrealistic summit.

D Aconcagua, South America (6,960m)

The original and now standard route up Aconcagua is little more than a walk. In January 1992, I arrived with my wife, Sharu, at Punta del Inca and was pleasantly surprised to meet fellow mountaineer and guide, Phil Erscheler. He was taking a party up the mountain via the Polish Glacier, away from the busy standard route, and suggested that we go with them.

After three days of sitting out bad weather, we left base camp. The Polish Glacier stretching up to the summit had been swept by vicious winds and glistened with pure ice. With a time limit to get back to Buenos Aires for our flight, we decided to miss out on the glacier. Instead we went across the north ridges towards the standard route and joined the large number of people wandering along the path. The wind was strong as we walked the last few metres to the summit and just before it got dark we camped outside the refuge.

Back at base camp we met eight members of the Jakarta Mountaineering Club. They were planning to climb the Seven Summits and felt, when they learnt that I had already climbed four, that I should do the same. This was the first time I had seriously thought about such goal-orientation – something I had previously tried to avoid.

E   Vinson Massif, Antarctica (4,897m)

When I learnt that climbing Vinson Massif was just a matter of guiding enough people in order to finance the cost of getting there, attempting all of the Seven Summits became a reality. Our team left Britain towards the end of November 1992 and travelled the thousands of kilometres to the South Pole. At this time of the year the sun is always well above the horizon, throughout the day and 'night', and when the wind stops blowing it is utterly quiet. As in other polar regions, in the keen, clean air, there is such an invigorating atmosphere that the spirits are raised just by being there. On December 7 we left camp and headed off towards the summit. Against expectations, with winds gusting at around 80 kms per hour and temperatures below minus 50°C, we all got to the top within 8 hours. Our elation was somewhat tempered by visibility being down to just a few metres in the storm.

F   Elbrus, Europe (5,633m)

Our team assembled in St Petersburg during the early summer of 1994. On our arrival at the settlement of Terskol, beneath Elbrus, a commission was demanded from our guide for bringing foreigners into the valley, though this was later waived.

After a few days' acclimatising, the group set off up Elbrus by cableway to 3,900m. From there we walked to the refuge at 4,200m. Two days later, the wind buffeted us as we crossed open slopes, some of them glassy ice. By mid-afternoon we reached what we thought was the summit. But we found there was another kilometre-long ridge to the actual summit. As night fell, we returned to the refuge and the next day descended this, fortunately extinct, volcano.

G   Carstensz Pyramid, Australasia (4,883m)

On our expedition to Carstensz we hoped not only to establish a new route but to spend as much time as possible with the aboriginal Dani people. The largest gold mine in the world is cutting into the mountain, regarded as sacred by the local tribespeople.

We had been warned that we might be taken hostage or even killed by bandits but, undeterred, we left our hut by mid-morning and walked down winding lanes towards the jungle. On May 12 we started climbing. The weather improved and two of the team hared ahead. We were slower, since Sharu was filming. Climbing in rock shoes, we reached the summit by 11 am.

I was given a standing ovation on this, my seventh summit. Mission accomplished!

PAPER 2   WRITING (2 hours)

Part 1

1 You are staying in Britain and in your free time you help a charity organisation which raises money for the local hospital. You and your friend, Maria, recently helped at a fund-raising day for this charity. Your friend has seen a newspaper report about the day, which she has sent to you because she feels it is inaccurate.

Read the newspaper report, on which your friend has made some notes, the letter from your friend, and the Distribution of Income pie chart you have prepared. Then, **using the information appropriately**, write a letter to the editor of the newspaper, giving the correct version of events and asking for an apology.

WASHOUT FOR CHARITY DAY

The charity day held in Cooper's Park on Saturday was not the success that the organisers had hoped for. To begin with, only 34 of the promised 45 stalls were there, so many visitors — *We only said 35* were disappointed. Then, the dance display and horse show were ruined by a sudden downpour of rain leaving many of the spectators cold and wet! — *No!! small shower, actually*

All this meant that the organisers did not reach their target figure and the hospital has lost out. It also seems that the cost — *wrong* of organising the day was so high that less than 60% of the money raised will go to the hospital. — *not true – you have the chart, don't you?*

Clearly, events like this need more careful planning in the future.

I have already written to the newspaper, but could you write as well as you were also at the day. They need to be told the true version. I really think they should apologise – in print! Bad publicity like this won't help the hospital.

Love,
Maria

CHARITY DAY RESULTS

Distribution of Income

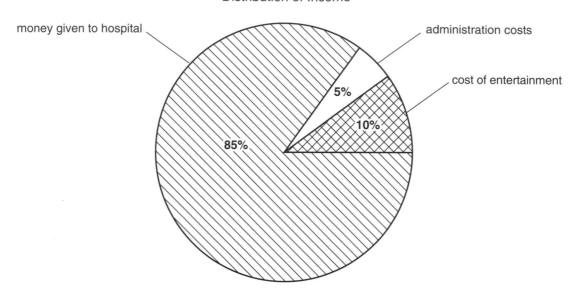

money given to hospital

administration costs

cost of entertainment

5%

10%

85%

Now write your **letter** to the editor of the newspaper (approximately 250 words). You do not need to include postal addresses. You should use your own words as far as possible.

Part 2

Choose **one** of the following writing tasks. Your answer should follow exactly the instructions given. Write approximately 250 words.

2   An international magazine has asked its readers to send in a review of **two** different computer games. Write a review for the magazine in which you compare and contrast **two** different computer games, commenting on the following points:

- graphics and visuals
- the appeal of each game
- value for money.

Write your **review**.

3   You see this competition in an international magazine.

> If you were able to travel back to any place and time in history, where and when would you choose?
>
> Describe what you might experience and tell us why you would choose this particular place and time.
>
> The most interesting entry will be published in the next issue.

Write your **competition entry**.

4   You see the following announcement in an international motoring magazine.

> ### HOW TO PASS YOUR DRIVING TEST
>
> We would like our readers around the world to share their ideas and experiences. Write us an article suggesting how best to prepare for a driving test, and saying what you should or should not do on the day of the test itself.

Write your **article**.

5   Your department recently put in a request for more office equipment, and received the following memo from the Managing Director.

> Re: your request for office equipment
>
> I need more information before I can make a decision. Could you write me a report stating what the limitations are of the equipment you currently use, and saying how this additional investment would improve your department's performance.

Write your **report**.

PAPER 3   ENGLISH IN USE (1 hour 30 minutes)

Part 1

For questions **1–15**, read the text below and then decide which word on page **95** best fits each space. Put the letter you choose for each question in the correct box on your answer sheet. The exercise begins with an example (**0**).

Example:

0	*B*	0

UNIVERSAL WET WEEKEND

The weather across much of the British Isles (**0**) ..... settled last week, with a good (**1**) ..... of sunshine. On Saturday, the lunchtime temperature at Bridlington on the north-east (**2**) ..... of England was 28.2°C, which compared favourably with Alicante in southern Spain at 29°C. The (**3**) ..... of the world, however, was coping with some (**4**) ..... conditions. A tropical storm, given the name Helen, hit Hong Kong on Saturday morning, though her presence had been (**5**) ..... in advance. From noon on Friday, the showers and (**6**) ..... of rain became more and more frequent so that by midnight on Sunday, thirty-six hours (**7**) ..... , there had been 333 mm of rainfall, not far off the (**8**) ..... for the month of August, at 367 mm. Even on Sunday there was a (**9**) ..... in Helen's tail. The town centre of Shanwei, near Hong Kong, was (**10**) ..... when 468 mm of rain fell in the sixty hours leading up to midday on Sunday, (**11**) ..... twice the normal August rainfall. On the other (**12**) ..... of the globe, tropical storm Gabrielle moved across the Gulf of Mexico and overnight rain (**13**) ..... the usual rainfall for the (**14**) ..... month. Although most of Europe enjoyed sun, the high temperatures were sufficient to set off some (**15**) ..... showers. On Tuesday morning, a thunderstorm at Lyons in eastern France deposited 99 mm of rain in just six hours.

0	**A**	kept	**(B)**	remained	**C**	lasted	**D**	held
1	**A**	extent	**B**	quantity	**C**	proportion	**D**	deal
2	**A**	shore	**B**	coast	**C**	sands	**D**	beach
3	**A**	residue	**B**	remnant	**C**	rest	**D**	remains
4	**A**	extreme	**B**	extravagant	**C**	excessive	**D**	exaggerated
5	**A**	waited	**B**	found	**C**	felt	**D**	warned
6	**A**	outbursts	**(B)**	outbreaks	**C**	outputs	**D**	outlets
7	**A**	after	**B**	plus	**C**	later	**D**	more
8	**A**	general	**B**	standard	**C**	medium	**D**	average
9	**A**	sting	**B**	prick	**C**	stab	**D**	poke
10	**A**	drowned	**B**	flooded	**C**	immersed	**D**	overflowed
11	**A**	only	**B**	fairly	**C**	hardly	**D**	nearly
12	**A**	section	**B**	side	**C**	face	**D**	part
13	**A**	overtook	**B**	exceeded	**C**	passed	**D**	beat
14	**A**	total	**B**	sole	**C**	single	**D**	whole
15	**A**	huge	**B**	weighty	**C**	heavy	**D**	strong

Part 2

For questions **16–30**, complete the following article by writing each missing word in the correct box on your answer sheet. **Use only one word for each space**. The exercise begins with an example (**0**).

Example: | 0 | *of* | 0 |

Travelling through Norway

The final part **(0)** ..... our journey started at Gudbrandsdalen, said by many to be the most beautiful of **(16)** ..... the valleys in Norway. **(17)** ..... was a wonderful landscape, the more so **(18)** ..... being dotted with centuries-old wooden farmhouses, scrupulously maintained in their original condition. At Ringebu the view broadened out and the first high peaks and glaciers came **(19)** ..... view. This view continued to dominate the trip as the train passed through the little village of Dovre, at the foot of the mountains which give this railway **(20)** ..... name – the Dovre Line. The village lies close **(21)** ..... the pretty village of Dombas, where the track divides. We were heading north, travelling **(22)** ..... a pass and descending into country **(23)** ..... was now more tundra-like, **(24)** ..... only occasional birch trees and mountain huts. From time to time we saw **(25)** ..... lone skier, and once we spotted a man fishing through a hole drilled in the ice. That made us think of food and we made **(26)** ..... way to the restaurant car. We continued through the tundra, the snow sometimes broken **(27)** ..... tracks of elk or reindeer. Although we were not lucky **(28)** ..... to see any, we **(29)** ..... see a pair of arctic hares later on. In no time at all, we found we **(30)** ..... arrived in Trondheim.

Part 3

In **most** lines of the following text, there is **one** unnecessary word. It is either grammatically incorrect or does not fit in with the sense of the text. For each numbered line **31–46**, find this word and then write it in the box on your answer sheet. **Some lines are correct**. Indicate these lines with a tick (✔) in the box. The exercise begins with two examples (**0**) and (**00**).

Examples:

0	*of*	0
00	✔	00

All-news Radio

0   In 1961, an eccentric but inspired American entrepreneur named of Gordan

00   McLendon carried out an experiment that involved beaming a high-powered

31   signal from Tijuana, Mexico to Los Angeles. Unlike any one other existing

32   radio station, McLendon's English-language station promised to provide for

33   nothing but news. Today, most US cities have at least one all-news radio

34   station. The largest cities have several in a competition and all of them follow

35   a similar pattern: headlines, sports, traffic, weather and business news, all

36   which delivered two or three times an hour. The statistics on all-news radio

37   are intriguing. Few Americans under 35 listen to news radio and the majority

38   of listeners are aged with 55 or over. Perhaps because of the popularity of

39   all-news TV stations, and at the expense of retaining large numbers of staff

40   such as reporters and presenters, the number of all-news radio stations is yet

41   declining in the US. But with the speed of communications are increasing,

42   the all-news radio format continues on to be one of the most profitable in the

43   US media business. One media critic has explained why its attraction in this

44   way: 'The main difference between the news services of radio, television and

45   newspapers is to do with the very immediacy of receiving the news item – on

46   the radio you can hear it now, on television you can see it just tonight, and

in the newspapers you can read it tomorrow.'

Part 4

For questions **47–61**, read the two texts on pages **98** and **99**. Use the words in the boxes to the right of the texts to form **one** word that fits in the same numbered space in the text. Write the new word in the correct box on your answer sheet. The exercise begins with an example (**0**).

Example:

0	*artistic*	0

BOOK EXTRACT

Being a Theatre Director

The director has overall responsibility for the **(0)** ..... side of a production and must conduct all the **(47)** ..... and keep an eye on all the backstage and technical departments involved.

Directors tend to have strong personalities and can be **(48)** ...... But the success or **(49)** ..... of a play is in their hands. It is their job to draw out the **(50)** ..... qualities in the actors in order to get the best **(51)** ..... from them. Some directors let actors decide on their own **(52)** ..... while others give detailed instructions as to how they want the parts to be played.

Some directors also take on **(53)** ..... duties, such as planning a season's programme and supervising the budget.

(0)	**ART**
(47)	REHEARSE
(48)	TEMPERAMENT
(49)	FAIL
(50)	IMAGINE
(51)	RESPOND
(52)	INTERPRET
(53)	MANAGER

BOOK REVIEW

World of Knowledge

This book breaks new ground in the **(54)** ..... method it uses to present information to the reader. The unique page design combines **(55)** ..... with an alphabetical reference section to provide an instant understanding of any topic, together with more in-depth treatment of the subject matter. At the foot of each page is a reference section, which gives articles which define or **(56)** ..... on the topic discussed. Within each reference section, the reader is directed to **(57)** ..... information through cross-referencing to other **(58)** ..... . The incomparable quality of the text and the **(59)** ..... of its presentation, ensure that this book can be read both for **(60)** ..... and for the most up-to-date **(61)** ..... of the subject.

(54)	DISTINCT
(55)	NARRATE
(56)	LARGE
(57)	FAR
(58)	ENTER
(59)	ORIGINAL
(60)	ENJOY
(61)	COVER

Part 5

For questions **62–74**, read the following letter from a Head of Department and use the information in it to complete the numbered gaps in the letter to a friend on page **101**. The words you need **do not** occur in the letter from the Head of Department. **Use no more than two words for each gap**. The exercise begins with an example (**0**).

Example:

0	*change*	0

LETTER FROM HEAD OF DEPARTMENT

Thank you for your letter regarding your wish to transfer to another course. I am pleased that you have informed me at this early stage of your concerns, but am of the opinion that you should allow yourself more time. In my experience new students often suffer from homesickness, but this disappears within a short period. I advise you to continue on the same programme for another two weeks and at the same time make an appointment to see your personal tutor to discuss matters in detail.

Should you finally decide to apply for a new programme, acceptance is conditional not only on whether there is a vacancy on the course of your choice, but also on whether you meet the course entry requirements.

Finally, I would say that once a decision is made you should take prompt action by first obtaining a letter of approval from your personal tutor. Making such a transfer should present no difficulties provided that it is made during the first term.

LETTER TO FRIEND

Dear Sue

I've been here a week and I'm afraid I've made an awful mistake.
I always wanted to study Law but I now realise it's not for me! I want to
(0) ..... my course if I can. I wrote to the Department Head. He was
glad that I'd let **(62)** ..... so early in the term about my **(63)** ..... .
However, he said I should **(64)** ..... bit longer to decide if I really want
to change. He thinks I may settle down because, he says, new
students often feel upset with the move away from their families – and
I do **(65)** ..... everybody at home. He says that this feeling will **(66)** .....
a short time. His **(67)** ..... that I carry on with Law for another **(68)** .....
weeks and, at the same time, arrange to see my personal tutor to
(69) ..... the whole thing.

If I do switch courses, I'll have to see if there's **(70)** ..... available and if
I'm good **(71)** ..... get on the course. Once I've made the decision, I'll
have to act quite **(72)** ..... and get my personal tutor to **(73)** ..... and
say that the move is OK. It should be **(74)** ..... I do it in the first term.

Part 6

For questions **75–80**, read the following text and then choose from the list **A–J** given below the best phrase to fill each of the spaces. Write one letter (**A–J**) in the correct box on your answer sheet. Each correct phrase may only be used once. **Some of the suggested answers do not fit at all.** The exercise begins with an example (**0**).

Example: | **0** | *J* | | **0** |

The art of conversation in the UK

You're having lunch with a friend in one of your favourite places to eat, there's nothing novel about the surroundings or the events that unfold around you, **(0)** ..... . This leaves you to concentrate on the conversation, **(75)** ..... , from movies and restaurants to politics and relationships. It's the usual sort of conversation the two of you have **(76)** ..... . But think about this: the two of you are able to talk continuously without ever giving a single thought to how you're able to do that.

Forget all the factors that might determine what you're going to discuss, like when you last got together **(77)** ..... . Just think about the mechanics of the conversation: the way that you take turns – you talk, **(78)** ..... . The most elementary aspect of a conversation is how these turns are taken but it is hard to say how this process actually works.

Obviously, you and your friend do take turns and those turns are beautifully choreographed. Long pauses are awkward, **(79)** ..... , very few gaps will appear in this conversation. Instead, you finish speaking, **(80)** ..... , your friend starts. Remember, in an hour-long lunch, that's a lot of precision switching back and forth. The puzzle is, how do the two of you manage it?

A and the signals dictated by those rules
B and there's little that's really surprising
C and without giving you time for a breath
D and how those topics are introduced
E and you and your friend cover all the topics you normally do
F and unless there's a great deal of strain in the relationship
G and then your friend talks, then you, then your friend
H and what's happening to both of you
I and the signals that you are sending to each other

J and you know the menu pretty well

PAPER 4   LISTENING (approximately 45 minutes)

Part 1

You will hear a talk on the radio given by an art teacher who became interested in making mosaics – designs made with small pieces of glass and stone. For questions **1–8**, complete the sentences.

You will hear the recording twice.

MOSAICS

The real experts in mosaics were [____ 1]

The greatest changes have occurred in the [____ 2] of mosaics.

Recently there was a possibility that mosaic-making would [____ 3]

To make mosaics, people must have enough [*and* 4]

Most students come to a [____ 5]

Making mosaics can be compared to doing [____ 6]

Mosaics are even appearing on [____ 7]

Once they are finished, mosaics continue to [____ 8]

for a long time.

Part 2

You will hear part of a radio programme in which someone is talking about summer courses at colleges and universities in Britain. For questions **9–16**, complete the sentences.

Listen very carefully as you will hear the recording ONCE only.

SUMMER COURSES

The minimum length of a course is [**9**]

One advantage is that students can study until late in [**10**]

For students on intensive courses [**11**] is provided.

Some students may consider the fully residential courses too [**12**]

The universities involved in the *Summer Academy* try to make full use of their [**13**]

On a few courses it is possible to receive [**14**]

One student's initial reason for going on a course was [**15**]

The student has now become a [**16**]

Part 3

You will hear part of a radio programme in which two people, Sally White and Martin Jones, are discussing the popularity of audio books (books recorded on tape), and the problems involved with abridging books before taping them. For questions **17–24**, choose the correct answer **A**, **B**, **C** or **D**.

You will hear the recording twice.

17 Sally thinks that most people listen to audio books

- **A** on the way to work.
- **B** when they're with their children.
- **C** when they're doing housework.
- **D** before they go to sleep.

18 Sally feels that the main advantage of audio books is that they

- **A** encourage children to read more.
- **B** make more books accessible to children.
- **C** save parents from having to read to children.
- **D** are read by experienced actors.

19 What does Martin say about the woman in the shop?

- **A** She no longer worries about long journeys.
- **B** Her children used to argue about what to listen to.
- **C** She no longer takes her children to France.
- **D** Her children don't like staying in hotels.

20 In the United States there is a demand for audio books because people there

- **A** were the first to obtain audio books.
- **B** have to drive long distances.
- **C** are used to listening to the spoken word on the radio.
- **D** feel that they do not have time to read books.

21 Authors may record their own books on tape if

- **A** their book has just been published.
- **B** they want it read a certain way.
- **C** they have already read extracts from it aloud.
- **D** there are no suitable actors available.

22 According to Sally, successful abridgements depend on

- **A** their closeness to the original.
- **B** the length of the original.
- **C** the style of the author.
- **D** the type of story.

23 Martin feels that unabridged versions

- **A** are better than abridgements.
- **B** can be too expensive.
- **C** are becoming more popular.
- **D** contain too much detail.

24 Books are not commissioned specifically for the audio market because

- **A** writers are too busy working for the BBC.
- **B** such books have failed in the past.
- **C** people only want familiar stories.
- **D** there are not enough people buying audio books.

Part 4

You will hear five short extracts in which different people are talking about the importance of eating breakfast.

You will hear the recording twice. While you listen you must complete both tasks.

TASK ONE

For questions **25–29**, match the extracts with the speakers, listed **A–H**.

A   stewardess

B   swimmer   **Speaker 1** | 25

C   researcher
                              Speaker 2 | 26
D   doctor

E   train driver   **Speaker 3** | 27

F   journalist
                              Speaker 4 | 28
G   athlete

H   teacher   **Speaker 5** | 29

TASK TWO

For questions **30–34**, match the extracts with the comments, listed **A–H**.

A   My job makes breakfast impossible.
                              Speaker 1 | 30
B   My advice is for adults.

C   My ideas are original.   **Speaker 2** | 31

D   My routine surprises people.
                              Speaker 3 | 32
E   My planning is worth it.

F   My work is respected.   **Speaker 4** | 33

G   My advice keeps changing.
                              Speaker 5 | 34
H   My experience supports a theory.

PAPER 5   SPEAKING (15 minutes)

There are two examiners. One (the Interlocutor) conducts the test, providing you with the necessary materials and explaining what you have to do. The other examiner (the Assessor) is introduced to you, but then takes no further part in the interaction.

Part 1 (3 minutes)

The Interlocutor first asks you and your partner a few questions. You are then asked to find out some information about each other, on topics such as hobbies, interests, future plans, etc. You are then asked further questions by the Interlocutor.

Part 2 (4 minutes)

You are each given the opportunity to talk for about a minute, and to comment briefly after your partner has spoken.

   The Interlocutor gives you a set of pictures and asks you to talk about them for about one minute. It is important to listen carefully to the Interlocutor's instructions. The Interlocutor then asks your partner a question about your pictures and your partner responds briefly.

   You are then given another set of pictures to look at. Your partner talks about these pictures for about one minute. This time the Interlocutor asks you a question about your partner's pictures and you respond briefly.

Part 3 (approximately 4 minutes)

In this part of the test you and your partner are asked to talk together. The Interlocutor places a new set of pictures on the table between you. This stimulus provides the basis for a discussion. The Interlocutor explains what you have to do.

Part 4 (approximately 4 minutes)

The Interlocutor asks some further questions, which leads to a more general discussion of what you have talked about in Part 3. You may comment on your partner's answers if you wish.

Test 1 Key

Paper 1   Reading (1 hour 15 minutes)

Part 1

1 B   2 D   3 A   4 D   5 B   6 C   7 A   8 E   9 D
10 B   11 C   12 A   13 D   14 B

Part 2

15 C   16 H   17 A   18 E   19 D   20 G   21 F

Part 3

22 C   23 A   24 B   25 D   26 A   27 C   28 B

Part 4

29 C   30 C   31 A   32 D   33 C   34 A   35 B
36 A   37 D   38 B   39 C   40 B   41 A   42 C
43 B   44 C   45 C   46 A   47 A

Paper 2   Writing (2 hours)

Task-specific mark schemes

Part 1

Question 1

Content (points covered)
For a mark of 3 or above, the candidate's **report** must:
• assess the advantages and/or disadvantages of the 3 proposals
• recommend 1 company
• justify their recommendation.

Organisation and cohesion
Clearly organised into paragraphs.
Report format; headings would be an advantage. Acceptable to use letter format.

Range
Language of explanation, evaluation and justification.
Vocabulary relating to canteen services.

Register
Consistently formal or unmarked.

Target Reader
Would have a clear idea of which company was recommended and why.

108

Part 2

Question 2

Content (points covered)
For a mark of 3 or above, the candidate's **article** must:
- outline the impact of new technology on their lives
- comment on future changes
- explain how these changes may affect them.

Organisation and cohesion
Clearly organised into paragraphs. Early mention of topic(s).

Range
Vocabulary relating to technology, language of explanation and speculation.

Register
Appropriately unmarked, informal or formal.

Target reader
Would be informed about the impact of technology on the candidate's life.

Question 3

Content (points covered)
For a mark of 3 or above, the candidate's **competition entry** must:
- explain why they agree or disagree with the statement
- refer to work, contact with native speakers and travel.

Organisation and cohesion
Clearly organised into paragraphs.

Range
Language of explanation and description, vocabulary relating to language learning.

Register
Consistently unmarked, informal or formal.

Target reader
Would have a clear understanding of candidate's point of view and would consider the entry.

Question 4

Content (points covered)
For a mark of 3 or above, the candidate's **account** must:
- explain why the event took place
- describe what happened
- make clear its effect on the candidate.

Organisation and cohesion
Clear paragraphing.

Range
Language of description and evaluation.

Register
Consistently formal, unmarked or informal.

Target reader
Would be informed and would consider the account for publication.

Question 5

Content (points covered)
For a mark of 3 or above, the candidate's **review** must:
- name the book
- give a summary of the contents
- describe what they learnt from the book
- explain how it may help others.

Organisation and Cohesion
Clear paragraphing. Early mention of title of book.

Range
Language of description, evaluation and recommendation. Vocabulary relating to work.

Register
Consistently formal or unmarked.

Target reader
Would be informed.

Paper 3 English in Use (1 hour 30 minutes)

Part 1

1 C   2 C   3 D   4 A   5 A   6 B   7 A   8 D   9 B   10 A
11 B   12 D   13 C   14 A   15 B

Part 2

16 to   17 as   18 so   19 be   20 Despite   21 like   22 in
23 this   24 have/cause/produce   25 which/that   26 no   27 it
28 such   29 how/why   30 more

Part 3

31 Austrian   32 machine   33 box. Alexander   34 materials, which   35 led
36 necessary   37 electronically   38 ✓   39 recently, the   40 ✓
41 however, there   42 ✓   43 talkers   44 current   45 device's   46 ✓

Part 4   (one mark for each correct section)

47 compositions   48 emphasis   49 practical   50 input(s)   51 connection(s)
52 treatment(s)   53 literary   54 widened   55 arrangements   56 overseas
57 dramatically   58 solution   59 independence   60 absence   61 flexibility

Part 5

62 reduced/special/cheap(er)/low(er)   63 date from/are from/come from/originate from
64 valuable/expensive/precious/antique   65 prohibited from/prevented from
66 fragile/delicate   67 photography/photographing   68 available/on sale/for sale/sold
69 to deposit/to leave   70 when entering/before entering/on entering
71 accidentally/inadvertently/unwittingly   72 to protect/to prevent/to keep
73 by daylight/by sunlight/by light   74 essential/vital/necessary/very important

NB The mark scheme for Part 5 may be expanded with other appropriate answers.

Part 6

75 D   76 A   77 G   78 C   79 H   80 F

Paper 4 Listening (45 minutes approximately)

Part 1

1 freedom (and) achievement (*either order*)   2 adventure sports   3 mental preparation
4 icefall/ice fall(s)/ice falling/falling ice/falls of ice   5 luxuries
6 (some/unnecessary/her) perfume   7 toothbrush   8 melted snow/(drinking) water
9 shared excitement   10 On Top of the World

Part 2

11 engineering   **12** industry   **13** hospital radio
14 rejection(s) (letters)/letters of rejection   **15** training (sessions)
16 three hours/3 hours   **17** opening (the/his) mail/letters
18 content   **19** music press/papers/newspapers/magazines

Part 3

20 C   **21** C   **22** D   **23** D   **24** A   **25** C

Part 4

26 B   **27** A   **28** C   **29** D   **30** G   **31** A   **32** H   **33** B   **34** C
35 E

Transcript   *This is the Cambridge Certificate in Advanced English Listening Test. Test One.*

This paper requires you to listen to a selection of recorded material and answer the accompanying questions.

*There are four parts to the test. You will hear Part Two **once** only. All the other parts of the test will be heard twice.*

There will be a pause before each part to allow you to look through the questions, and other pauses to let you think about your answers. At the end of every pause, you will hear this sound.

tone

*You should write your answers in the spaces provided on the **question paper**. You will have **ten** minutes at the end to **transfer your answers to the separate answer sheet**.*

There will now be a pause. You must ask any questions now as you will not be allowed to speak during the test.

[pause]

PART 1   *Now open your question paper and look at Part One.*

[pause]

You will hear a talk given by a woman who is a successful climber. For questions 1 to 10, complete the sentences. You will hear the recording twice. You now have 30 seconds to look at Part 1.

[pause]

tone

Climber: People often ask me when I was first bitten by the climbing bug. Well, it happened when, as a journalist, I accompanied an Anglo-American expedition on Everest's North East ridge in 1989. I went there with no intention other than to write about other people climbing the mountain. I wanted to see what made mountaineers tick, why they gave up jobs and left their families just to climb a hill! Over the

112

couple of months I spent with the expedition, I began to understand the sense of freedom and achievement of mountaineering and did lots of learning and exploration. I think they were the happiest two months of my life.

Over the next three and a half years I honed my newly-acquired climbing skills on various mountains all over the world. People say 'Weren't your family surprised by this new interest?' Well, they weren't, because I'd already done numerous other what people like to call 'adventure sports', like hang-gliding and scuba diving. Anyway, in 1993, my hobby got completely out of hand! I gave up my job, let out my flat and joined the British Everest Expedition. To prepare physically for it, I trained at my local gym. The mental preparation, however, was much more difficult. There were lots of things that frightened me about Everest. One of them was the icefall that you have to climb through. A friend asked if there was any way I could prepare myself for it. I thought: 'What can I do – put myself in a fridge and look at lumps of ice?'

Everest is certainly not a place for cowards, and it's also certainly not a place for life's luxuries. You don't carry anything that isn't necessary because weight multiplies at high altitudes. The first time I went to Everest, as a journalist, I carried my perfume all the way. I soon realised that it was unnecessary. You can forget baths and showers on a mountain as well. I didn't even take my toothbrush higher than 7,000 metres. It's not through uncleanliness or laziness that you don't wash, it's through sheer practicality. The only source of water is melted snow. To melt snow you need fuel and fuel is heavy, so you don't melt snow unless you're going to drink it.

The question I'm asked most often is, 'How did you feel when you reached the summit?' Well, I still get emotional when I think about it. It was fabulous because neither of the two sherpas with me had been to the top before either. There was this tremendous feeling of shared excitement.

Since then, I've gone on to climb a number of other summits and I plan to tackle Mount Fuji later this year. And of course I've got my new career in TV – as a presenter on 'Tomorrow's World'. I'm in demand on the lecturing circuit and my book about my ascent of Everest – *On Top of the World* – is a best-seller. So, that's my story. Now, does anybody have any questions?

[pause]

tone

Now you will hear the recording again.

[The recording is repeated.]

[pause]

That is the end of Part One.

[pause]

PART 2

Part Two
You will hear a radio music presenter talking about his job. For questions 11 to 19, complete the sentences. Listen very carefully as you will hear the recording ONCE only. You now have 45 seconds to look at Part 2.

[pause]

tone

Q p26

Presenter:	I'd always wanted to work in radio but at first I didn't imagine it as a full-time career. After I got my engineering degree at university, I decided to go into industry. I think the experience gained outside radio has been to my advantage, so I have no regrets about doing engineering, or about working for a short time in industry. And during that period, I got my first taste of broadcasting, working for a hospital radio station.

The work was excellent training. I decided I wanted to become a music presenter professionally while I was doing that, and sent out hundreds of letters and audition tapes, which were all met with rejection. My advice to anyone trying to get into radio is to 'keep at it'. There are bound to be moments of despair as the rejection letters pour in, but determination is the only way to succeed. Competition for music presenters' jobs is extremely tough – there are thousands of would-be disc jockeys around the country.

Anyway, eventually one station offered me a series of training sessions. As a result of these training sessions, I landed myself a part-time job on an overnight programme. Then I was offered some holiday relief work, which I managed to fit in with my holiday from my full-time job. A few months later I was offered a full-time presenter's job, which I took.

There's no such thing as a typical day in radio. My schedule depends on how many programmes I'm responsible for in any one week. Generally, I have a three-hour afternoon programme six days a week. I usually arrive at 9.30 and spend the first hour opening mail – I get a lot of mail and I have to make arrangements for it to be answered. Then I concentrate on the content of that afternoon's programme. When I've decided on the content, I plan the running order. After lunch, I usually spend the time before going on air scanning the music press – I often find interesting stories I can use on the programme in the music press. Sometimes in this period before my programme begins I record advertisements for the station. My programme runs from 3 pm till 6 pm. When it's all over, I clear away the records and usually set off home by 6.30 pm.

[pause]

That is the end of Part Two.

[pause]

PART 3	*Part Three*
	You will hear part of an interview with someone who founded a magazine. For questions 20 to 25, choose the correct answer A, B, C or D. You will hear the recording twice. You now have one minute to look at Part Three.

[pause]

tone

Interviewer:	… OK, welcome back to the programme. Well, for the hundred thousand or more people in London who buy every issue, *Time Out* is an invaluable guide to what's going on in the city. In its lists they can find everything from films, plays, concerts and night clubs to exhibitions, sports, opera, dance and special events. And I'm talking now to Tony Elliott, the man who started it all, back in 1968. Tony, what gave you the idea?
Tony Elliott:	Well, back then it was very hard to find out about those things. There were magazines, there was a magazine called *What's On*, which was a weekly, which

is still around, rather, kind of, conventional in its approach, and you could look in the evening paper or you could look in the music press, um, to get information, but nothing covered everything all in one place. Um, so I perceived there was a gap and I suppose to some extent I just produced a magazine for myself, and it turned out a lot of other people wanted the same thing.

Interviewer: At first, the magazine was just a sheet sold hand to hand in the street, wasn't it?

Tony Elliott: Well, I started with a few like-minded people and we did actually put it into newsagents – people do seem to think we started as a bunch of idealistic amateurs, but I have to say that I think we were actually pretty professional from day one. It was coming out every three weeks so I'd spend three or four days actually going round something like 300 newsagents. The selling in the street was partly to do with getting copies sold so that we actually had some cash but it also had this kind of in-built market research thing where you'd show people what you were doing and they'd go 'Oh really' and a lot of people said, 'Oh, that's a modern *What's On*, that's what we've been looking for.'

Interviewer: So, did you have any publishing experience before this?

Tony Elliott: Mmm, I did a regular column for a magazine at university which was quite serious. It used to do single themes per issue, like provincial theatre or education or racialism, and then when I took it over I promptly changed it into being a kind of contemporary arts magazine. We did interviews with artists, rock stars, writers, people like that.

Interviewer: Were you still at university when you started *Time Out*?

Tony Elliott: Yeah, technically I was actually on holiday for the summer vacation, and as far as the university was concerned I was supposed to be going to France to teach. I think I'd told them I would do, because, you know, you go away for a term or a year if you're studying French, and um, then I just started doing the magazine.

Interviewer: And, er, didn't go back.

Tony Elliott: Yes, well there was a point when I suddenly realised that I was doing what I wanted to do.

Interviewer: So it soon took off, didn't it? I mean it was monthly first and then it went weekly, didn't it, in a very short time?

Tony Elliott: Well, it started monthly and then we went three-weekly – for some reason that was the highest frequency we could do. Then we went fortnightly, which is quite a valid frequency for publication, and then inevitably we went weekly – stimulated, I have to say, by the threat of some competition from some people who were starting a similar publication.

Interviewer: Oh, yes, I was going to say, someone else must have spotted the gap, I mean you identified it, but there must have been big publishing houses who thought, 'Hang on, we can have some of this too'.

Tony Elliott: I think the truth is nobody really realised what the significance of the magazine was, 'cos in a sense it started very tiny, very small, and then built up and built up and a lot of publishers and a lot of advertisers also were very, um, dismissive of our readers. I mean, still, even today, you get occasional accusations like 'It's not a particularly significant readership' and 'A lot of students read it, don't they?' and things like that. People just didn't realise that, um, that we were creating a readership that was very significant.

Interviewer: The readership's grown up with you as well, hasn't it? A lot of people I imagine who were buying it as students in the Sixties are now buying it as parents of teenage children these days.

Tony Elliott:	That would imply our readership's now older, which isn't the case. And although the numbers have expanded, well it's true that there are more people over 35 buying it than there were when it started, the readership hasn't really changed, it's still basically intelligent young people who do things.
Interviewer:	OK, well, we'll take a quick break now and then I'll be back to talk to Tony some more …

[pause]

tone

Now you will hear the recording again.

[The recording is repeated.]

[pause]

That is the end of Part Three.

[pause]

PART 4

Now look at the fourth and last part of the test. Part 4 consists of two tasks.

You will hear five short extracts in which different people are talking about things that have recently happened at work. Look at Task One. For questions 26 to 30, match the extracts with the situations, listed A to H. Now look at Task Two. For questions 31 to 35, match the extracts with the feeling each speaker expresses, listed A to H.

You will hear the recording twice. While you listen you must complete both tasks. You now have 40 seconds in which to look at Part 4.

[pause]

tone

Speaker One:	So the Head of Department called me in and launched into this long speech about how my messing up the arrangements for his meeting had created all sorts of trouble for him. While he was going on about it, I glanced at the bit of paper in front of him and I saw the signature and I realised it hadn't been me. I knew it wasn't like me anyway, I mean, I get things wrong but only trivial things. It's going to be hilarious when he realises what a fool he's made of himself. I doubt I'll be able to keep a straight face.
Speaker Two:	Yeah, I was busy and the Area Manager turned up. Well, I wasn't exactly thrilled to see him, it's hardly ever good news. Anyway, he wanted me to start on some other project. I'd been warned that was coming so I didn't have much trouble coming up with reasons for turning it down. He said I'd regret it later but I said I didn't think so, and he left it at that. The thing is, after all these years with the firm, all I get asked to do are the things no-one else fancies. It's really got me down – I joined with such high hopes and now I'm so disheartened, it's such a shame.
Speaker Three:	The ridiculous thing is, I'd always known she couldn't be trusted, but it's in my nature, I guess, to speak my mind. Still, I shouldn't have confided in her what I really thought of the job. It's just that when she asked me, it caught me unawares. It's got me into a lot of trouble now, because of course she's spread it round everyone else. I should just laugh it off, but that's easier said than done. She'd

better not come near me for a while, the way I feel I'd give her a piece of my mind. It infuriates me when people do that kind of thing.

Speaker Four: Jack came to my office today – we used to get on really well till they moved him upstairs and I hardly see him now – and he said, 'Hey, there's an opening in our office now. I've fixed it so you can have it.' Well, I didn't know what to say, it came right out of the blue. I mean, he's always done me favours and been kind to me but I can't think of anything worse than working there. So I feel awful about letting him down after all he's done for me, but I'm going to turn it down because it's my career, isn't it?

Speaker Five: Well, I tried to be my usual tactful self but he took offence. 'So you can't bear to come on this trip with me?' he asked and I said, 'It's not that, it's just that I've been to so many conferences lately, I want a break from them'. And he said, 'But this is the most important of the lot, don't be so stupid'. If I'd reacted to that, we'd have had an enormous row, so I didn't bother. That's the sort of thing that tends to happen with him. He's either all over you or he can't stand you. That's just the way it is – I won't let it bother me, what would be the point? There's nothing I can do about it.

[pause]

tone

Now you will hear the recording again. Remember you must complete both tasks.

[The recording is repeated.]

[pause]

*That is the end of Part Four. There will now be a ten-minute pause to allow you to **transfer your answers to the separate answer sheet**. Be sure to follow the numbering of all the questions. The question papers and answer sheets will then be collected by your supervisor.*

[Teacher, pause the tape here for ten minutes. Remind your students when they have one minute left.]

That is the end of the test.

Test 2 Key

Paper 1   Reading (1 hour 15 minutes)

Part 1

1 C/D   2 C/D   3 D   4 E   5 A   6 B   7 A   8 A/C   9 A/C
10 B/E   11 B/E   12 D   13 A   14 A/C   15 A/C   16 B

Part 2

17 D   18 A   19 G   20 E   21 B   22 C

Part 3

23 C   24 A   25 C   26 B   27 C   28 A   29 D

Part 4

30 A   31 E   32 A   33 D   34 B   35 F
36 D   37 A/B   38 A/B   39 A   40 D   41 F   42 B/C
43 B/C   44 F   45 D

Paper 2   Writing (2 hours)

Task-specific mark schemes

Part 1
Question 1
Content (points covered)
For Band 3 or above, the candidate's **letter** must:
• refer to newspaper article
• give a brief apology to local residents
• provide some information about college open day
• invite/persuade people to attend.

Organisation and cohesion
Letter layout with appropriate opening and closing formulae.

Range
Language of apology and persuasion.

Register
Consistently formal or unmarked.

Target reader
Would be informed about the college and consider printing the letter in the newspaper.

Part 2

Question 2

Content (points covered)
For Band 3 or above, the candidate's **proposal** must:
- give a reason for starting the magazine
- suggest some contents for first issue
- state what support and/or financial help is needed.

Organisation and cohesion
Clearly organised into sections/paragraphs. Letter/memo format acceptable.

Range
Vocabulary relating to magazines/writing.
Language of persuasion, explanation and justification.

Register
Consistently unmarked or formal.

Target reader
Would be informed about the reasons why a magazine was needed and consider supporting the idea.

Question 3

Content (points covered)
For Band 3 or above, the candidate's **competition entry** must describe benefits of:
- travelling alone
- travelling with friends
- travelling with family.

Organisation and cohesion
Clearly organised into paragraphs.

Range
Vocabulary relating to travel. Language of evaluation and assessment.

Register
Any, as long as consistent.

Target reader
Would consider the entry.

Question 4

Content (points covered)
For Band 3 or above, the candidate's **report** must refer to:
- measures being taken
- their success
- what more could be done with reference to their region.

Organisation and cohesion
Clearly organised in paragraphs. Use of headings desirable.

Range
Vocabulary relating to energy and natural resources. Language of evaluation and recommendation.

Register
Consistently formal or unmarked.

Target reader
Would be informed of the measures in place and future requirements.

Question 5

Content (points covered)
For Band 3 or above, the candidate's **character reference** must:
- indicate the length of time and in what capacity he/she has worked with applicant
- comment on applicant's business skills and experience
- mention some additional relevant personal qualities.

Organisation and cohesion
Clear layout and organisation with appropriate paragraphing. Letter/memo format acceptable.

Range
Language of business relationships. Marketing terms. Character description.

Register
Consistently formal or unmarked.

Target reader
Would be informed about the candidate.

Paper 3 English in Use (1 hour 30 minutes)

Part 1

1 C	2 B	3 B	4 D	5 A	6 B	7 D	8 B	9 D
10 A	11 B	12 C	13 C	14 A	15 C			

Part 2

16 same **17** an **18** in **19** This/That/It **20** would/could/might/may/must
21 so **22** or **23** there **24** rather/sooner **25** of **26** since **27** before
28 from **29** for/to/in **30** if

Part 3

31 only **32** then **33** been **34** ✓ **35** up **36** both **37** ✓ **38** had
39 ✓ **40** being **41** as **42** out **43** ✓ **44** of **45** itself
46 therefore

Part 4

47 freshness **48** simplicity **49** creative **50** ensure **51** numerous
52 delightful **53** varieties/variety **54** validated **55** requirements
56 prospective **57** successfully **58** choice **59** lecturers **60** daily
61 financially

Part 5

62 decision(s) **63** decorate/redecorate/renovate/refurbish **64** start date/starting date
65 calculated/estimated/predicted/told us/informed us **66** unavoidable/inevitable
67 progress/hand **68** apologize for **69** slightest/smallest **70** welcome/appreciate
71 doubt/doubts/fears **72** surroundings/conditions/work(ing) conditions
73 opinion(s)/suggestion(s)/idea(s)/preference(s) **74** hesitate to

NB The mark scheme for Part 5 may be expanded with other appropriate answers.

Part 6

75 H **76** G **77** B **78** F **79** D **80** C

Paper 4   Listening (45 minutes approximately)

Part 1

1 wall **2** 79/seventy-nine **3** establish their position **4** treasure
5 exciting discoveries **6** a/every year **7** history of the site/site history
8 life in the town **9** dangerous walls/keep children off walls

Part 2

10 two/2 years/other year/second year **11** mixed voice
12 (an/the/their) application form **13** March to/–May **14** semi (-) final(s)
15 sing better/perform better/do better/(are) not put off **16** music stand
17 (new) equipment (for the choir)

Part 3

18 more flexibility   **19** competitive   **20** well-designed/planned/organised
21 (a lot of) surveys   **22** work at/from home/stay at home
23 socialising/socializing   **24** life skills   **25** friends/friendships

Part 4

26 G   **27** A   **28** E   **29** D   **30** C   **31** D   **32** A   **33** C
34 F   **35** H

Transcript *This is the Cambridge Certificate in Advanced English Listening Test. Test Two.*

This paper requires you to listen to a selection of recorded material and answer the accompanying questions.

*There are four parts to the test. You will hear Part Two **once** only. All the other parts of the test will be heard twice.*

There will be a pause before each part to allow you to look through the questions, and other pauses to let you think about your answers. At the end of every pause, you will hear this sound.

tone

*You should write your answers in the spaces provided on the **question paper**. You will have **ten** minutes at the end to **transfer your answers to the separate answer sheet.***

There will now be a pause. You must ask any questions now as you will not be allowed to speak during the test.

[pause]

PART 1 *Now open your question paper and look at Part One.*

[pause]

You will hear a guide speaking to tourists who are visiting some Roman remains. For questions 1 to 9, complete the sentences. You will hear the recording twice. You now have 30 seconds to look at Part 1.

[pause]

tone

Guide: Good morning and welcome to this morning's guided tour of the Roman remains in the area. We'll start our day by visiting the garrison town of Corbridge – then, this afternoon, we'll be visiting part of the wall which the Romans built to keep their enemies out of the country. The part we're going to visit is remarkably well-preserved and it's easy to imagine what it must have been like all those years ago!
   The Romans actually arrived in this country in the earlier part of the first century AD, but it wasn't until the year 79 that they came to the Corbridge area. They built

a series of forts and strongholds so that they could establish their position in the whole region.

What you're going to see this morning are the results of excavations which've taken place fairly recently. The first early archaeological dig was as far back as 1201 and then, believe it or not, they were looking for treasure. Unfortunately, (or perhaps fortunately for us!), nothing interesting was found, so they abandoned the site and it wasn't until the early nineteenth century that another, and much more ambitious, excavation was carried out.

The result was a number of exciting discoveries. And in the mid-nineteenth century, they discovered part of a Roman bridge and other structures, including the baths and other dwellings in the town. More recently, in fact every year since 1934, digs have taken place. These have resulted in the discovery of a large collection of sculpture, coins, pottery and small objects; and some of these have become very famous indeed. Most of them are now housed in the site museum, which we'll be visiting before we visit the site itself. Unfortunately, for security reasons, some have had to be taken to the city museum, which you'll find is about 15 miles away.

As you can see from this map, the site museum's laid out in a circle. The first half concentrates on the history of the site, and each section deals with er ... well, a separate period of the site's history. You'll also find display cases of objects which would've been in use at the time. In the second half of the museum, each section's related to a particular aspect of life in the town, such as trade, domestic life and religious observance.

After visiting the museum we'll be walking round the site, and we would ask you please, to pay particular attention to any loose stones lying around the site. And keep children off the walls, as these can be extremely dangerous. At the end of the tour we'll be paying a visit to the gift shop and café, which you probably saw as you came in – near the site entrance and the car park.

Now, if you've left hats and sunglasses in the coach, I'd advise you to go and retrieve them now as the coach'll be locked for the next few hours and the sun's very hot today.

[pause]

tone

Now you will hear the recording again.

[The recording is repeated.]

[pause]

That is the end of Part One.

[pause]

PART 2

Part Two
You will hear part of a radio programme in which someone is talking about a competition for choirs, or groups of singers. For questions 10 to 17, fill in the missing information. Listen very carefully as you will hear the recording ONCE only. You now have 45 seconds to look at Part 2.

[pause]

tone

Interviewer:	Kathy Lyle is Competition Manager for the Choir of the Year competition and she's in the studio with me now. Hi, Kathy.
Kathy Lyle:	Hello there.
Interviewer:	Is this something you get involved with annually then?
Kathy Lyle:	Well, actually, it's a biennial competition. The first competition was in 1984 and they've been running every second year since then.

There's actually four titles to be won. There's a title for each category, and we've got three categories: Youth Choirs, where the majority of the members are aged 16 or below; Mixed Voice Choirs whose members may have soprano, bass, tenor, any kind of voice; and then we've got the third category which is a Single Voice category, either for men's or women's voices. Then we have the champion of champions. One choir out of the three will be Choir of the Year.

The closing date is 22nd January so there's still time to get an application in. You don't need to send in a tape or anything like that, just an application form. Get the form back to me and provided the choir meets our requirements, being amateur is the main one, we'll give them an audition – a chance to show what they can do.

In the audition period that runs from March to May, we go all over the country and, obviously, our primary concern is finding top-quality choral music. We'll be touring the country from March onwards, auditioning the choirs that have applied and whittling it down to eight choirs in each category for the televised finals at the end of May.

For anyone who's worried about TV coverage, that only comes in from the semi-final stage of the competition onwards. All that happens is the choirs go out and do their stuff, and the cameramen move silently and smoothly around them, getting the best shots and really it adds a little to the occasion, but it doesn't tend to put people off, in fact it usually helps them perform better.

As for prizes, each of the category-winning choirs will receive a very nice, specially made music stand. So every time they look at the conductor in future, they'll be reminded of their success in the competition. In addition to that, the overall winner will receive a further £1000 with which to buy new equipment for the choir. So, there's quite a lot to sing for, and something new for the choir in the future as well.

Interviewer:	Kathy, it all sounds really exciting. Now if anyone out there sings in a choir and would like …

[pause]

That is the end of Part Two.

[pause]

PART 3   *Part Three*
You will hear a radio discussion about an office practice called 'hot desking'. For questions 18 to 25, complete the sentences. You will hear the recording twice. You now have one minute to look at Part 3.

[pause]

tone

Interviewer:	No more personal space, no papers strewn around, no more half-empty coffee cups or pictures of the kids. The modern office has embraced the concept of 'hot desking'. Hot desking means no regular desk to call your own, just a locker for your things and a rush each morning to claim your desk for the day. I have with me, Peter Potter, hot desker himself in a large multinational company and Lois Coleshill, a Personnel Officer who's distinctly lukewarm about the idea. Peter, tell us how it works.
Peter:	Well, we share a space, in our little group, where we're able to plug in our portable computers; we have telephones with code numbers so that we can have our calls redirected to whichever desk we happen to be at, and it allows us to work in a very flexible way. We can decide where we wish to work on any particular day and take our work with us.
Interviewer:	And Lois, why do you think this wouldn't work?
Lois:	I have a lot of concerns about what hot desking would actually mean for many people. For example, in a lot of companies with hot desking, it becomes very competitive about who gets the best desks. Our experience is that it's the people, for example, who are best able to leave home early in the morning who grab the best desk.
Peter:	I mean, who cares? It isn't really a matter of whether you get the best desk or not. I mean, there are many more important things at stake in a busy office than that. A well-designed office shouldn't have a best desk in any case. There's no reason why they shouldn't all be the same.
Lois:	Well, I'm sorry, people care terribly. One of the things, I mean, I've done quite a lot of surveys, asking people about what they want from work, and they've shown that things about the work environment, things like who you sit next to at work, or is it by the window, is it noisy and all those things are tremendously important to workers.
Interviewer:	Doesn't that present you with a problem, Peter, that it goes against those feelings?
Peter:	I think our experience is that the advantage it gives people is that it enables them to plan their day in such a way that actually being in the office becomes largely immaterial. For example, if I need to stay at home for a morning, I'm able to plug into the computer network from home, I don't need to go into the office at all.
Interviewer:	So, isn't Peter talking about something that gives people greater freedom?
Lois:	That's fine if you're talking about what Peter's talking about, which is people who have portable computers and can work from home, but a lot of companies that talk about hot desking aren't companies like that, they're companies where you have to be in the office. One of the things that's leading to a lot of job insecurity now amongst people is the extent to which we have lost the socialising role of the workplace. Workers are becoming more isolated and that's quite worrying.
Peter:	I think that's a view I have to echo; we still have to ensure that we build office environments in which people can fully socialise and feel a full part of. We have a team area for that reason, and people do keep their personal things there.

Lois: I'm still very unconvinced by hot desking. I mean the whole way in which work is becoming much more flexible and less collective is actually quite a concern because for many young people the workplace has been where people go to learn how to deal with other people, learn life skills, as opposed to work skills, especially as people seem to be working longer and longer hours and work takes up more of their lives. I think it's terribly sad if the workplace is becoming dehumanised; it's a real worry for me.

Peter: Well, I think you're probably overstating the case rather there, actually. Hot desking is about the efficient organisation of space and time; there's no reason why it should lead people to be less sociable. It certainly hasn't in our office. You get to sit next to different people, rather than the same person all the time, so you get to make new friends.

Lois: But it's the loss of security that upsets people, it's the not knowing how things are going to be, or where you're going to end up each day. People do find it very upsetting.

Peter: I think it probably just depends on the person then, because none of us feels that.

Lois: I think we must inhabit very different worlds actually.

Interviewer: Lois, Peter, I'm afraid that's all we have time for today.

[pause]

tone

Now you will hear the recording again.

[The recording is repeated.]

[pause]

That is the end of Part Three.

[pause]

PART 4   *Now look at the fourth and last part of the test. Part 4 consists of two tasks.*

You will hear five short extracts in which different people are talking about weekend activities. Look at Task One. For questions 26 to 30, match the extracts with the different activities, listed A to H. Now look at Task Two. For questions 31 to 35, match the extracts with the opinion each speaker expresses about the activity, listed A to H.

You will hear the recording twice. While you listen you must complete both tasks. You now have 40 seconds in which to look at Part 4.

[pause]

tone

Speaker 1: Well, we got there late unfortunately. The problem was that Dave couldn't find a parking space anywhere. We drove around for ages. I don't think we realised just how popular it was going to be. We nearly didn't bother you know. Last month's was such a disappointment – there wasn't much to see and not many people turned up. But this time it was the complete opposite. There were all kinds of food, a huge fish section, clothes, miscellaneous stalls with goodness knows what. Apart from it being almost impossible to make progress past the stalls we quite enjoyed it.

Speaker 2: Yes, Pete and I go quite regularly now. He wasn't too keen to begin with but over the last few months we've both got completely hooked. However, we were a bit unlucky last weekend. We were expecting great things and we'd been looking forward to it for ages. This was going to be the big one. We set off early, got the gear ready the night before, but after a couple of hours the weather set in. Couldn't see a thing. The visibility was down to about ten metres. There was no way we were going to reach the summit so we just had to abandon it. Discovered we'd lost one of our ropes when we got back home, just to cap it all.

Speaker 3: I haven't been for ages. It was a real treat for me. Of course, before I was married I used to go several times a year, but I don't think I've been now since nineteen ninety-four. It's not that my wife objects to it, it's just, well, I don't know. I suppose I feel a bit guilty going off at the weekend. But it's good fun – I love seeing all the big names. Mind you, not a lot happened. Nothing to clap or cheer about, but it didn't seem to matter. It was just being there, encouraging the players and despairing when they got it all wrong.

Speaker 4: We felt it was a good opportunity to celebrate. Occasions like this don't happen every day and everyone was in a good mood so we thought why not? The thing is we wanted it to be different, something that we'd always remember, something to round off a perfect day. Jamie had heard about this interesting place by the harbour where you sat on cushions and you prepared your own dishes. It sounded different so we set off for there. When we arrived the manager had already heard about our success and even though he was busy, he still managed to find plenty of room for us all.

Speaker 5: I was on my own at the weekend and I suppose I was a bit restless. You know, I've been working hard recently. I needed to get out in the fresh air and so I just headed off into the country. It was great – a beautiful day. It reminded me of when my father used to take me fishing. Well – I fancied a quick dip and so, as no-one was around, I just stripped off and plunged in. It was marvellous, but I got a bit over ambitious. Before I knew it, I was more than a mile out. It took me a very long time to get back and when I reached the shore again I lay in the sun for ages to get my breath back.

[pause]

tone

Now you will hear the recording again. Remember you must complete both tasks.

[The recording is repeated.]

[pause]

*That is the end of Part Four. There will now be a ten-minute pause to allow you to **transfer your answers to the separate answer sheet**. Be sure to follow the numbering of all the questions. The question papers and answer sheets will then be collected by your supervisor.*

[Teacher, pause the tape here for ten minutes. Remind your students when they have one minute left.]

That is the end of the test.

Test 3 Key

Paper 1 Reading (1 hour 15 minutes)

Part 1

1 C   2 B   3 A   4 C   5 B   6 C   7 D   8 A   9 A
10 D   11 B   12 C   13 A   14 D   15 C   16 A

Part 2

17 D   18 G   19 F   20 A   21 B   22 E

Part 3

23 D   24 B   25 B   26 C   27 B   28 A   29 A

Part 4

30 E   31 B   32 E   33 A   34 A/D   35 A/D   36 E   37 C/D
38 C/D   39 A   40 C/D   41 C/D   42 E   43 D   44 B/C   45 B/C
46 B   47 E   48 B

Paper 2 Writing (2 hours)

Task-specific mark schemes

Part 1

Question 1

Content (points covered)
For Band 3 or above, the candidate's **letter** to the Principal must:
• comment on his/her plans for changes to the sports centre
• offer the student committee's suggestions.

Agreement or disagreement with the plan is acceptable.

Organisation and cohesion
Letter layout with appropriate opening and closing formulae.
Clear organisation with appropriate paragraphing.
Memo format acceptable.

Range
Language of evaluation/comparison, explanation, agreement/disagreement.

Register
Consistently formal or unmarked.

Target reader
Would be informed of the student committee's views.

Part 2
Question 2
Content (points covered)
For Band 3 or above, the candidate's **article** must:
- name a representative of their country. (Fictional/legendary character would be acceptable.)
- explain why s/he attracts attention
- give an opinion about the person's image.

Organisation and cohesion
Clear organisation with appropriate paragraphing.

Range
Language of description, opinion.

Register
Any, as long as consistent.

Target reader
Would know who the representative was and why they were famous.

Question 3
Content (points covered)
For Band 3 or above, the candidate's **leaflet** must:
- describe a minimum of 2 ways of learning English independently.

Organisation and cohesion
Clear sections/paragraphs.
Coherent and cohesive explanation. Headings would be an advantage.

Range
Vocabulary related to language learning. Expressions of advice/recommendation.

Register
Any, as long as consistent.

Target reader
Would be informed about ways of learning English independently.

Question 4
Content (points covered)
For Band 3 or above, the candidate's **report** must:
- describe changes in attitude to at least 2 jobs/employment in general
- explain the reason for these changes in attitude
- predict possible future changes.

Organisation and cohesion
Report format. Headings an advantage. Clearly organised into paragraphs. Memo format acceptable.

Range
Vocabulary associated with work. Language of evaluation.

Register
Consistently formal or unmarked.

Target reader
Would be informed.

Question 5
Content (points covered)
For Band 3 or above, the candidate's **proposal** must:
- suggest which staff/group of staff should be re-deployed
- explain the sort of re-training needed
- state how long the re-training will take
- describe the benefits to the company/department.

Organisation and cohesion
Clear organisation with appropriate paragraphing. Memo format acceptable.

Range
Vocabulary related to business. Language of suggestion/recommendation.

Register
Consistently formal or unmarked.

Target reader
Would be informed of staffing and training needs in the company/department.

Paper 3   English in Use (1 hour 30 minutes)

Part 1

1 C   2 B   3 A   4 B   5 C   6 B   7 D   8 C   9 A
10 D   11 B   12 B   13 D   14 C   15 A

Part 2

16 where   17 this   18 whose   19 them/these   20 which/and
21 becoming/getting   22 despite   23 everything/anything/whatever
24 for   25 addition   26 all/half   27 One   28 off/from/on   29 with
30 themselves

Part 3

31 friend   32 ✓   33 disguised   34 ✓   35 Their   36 factors
37 desirable. Heinz   38 another   39 ketchup,   40 ✓   41 huge
42 business   43 ✓   44 its   45 through   46 tradesmen's

Part 4

47 universal   48 amazingly   49 hopeful/hopeless   50 countless   51 ability
52 insufficient   53 basics   54 foundation   55 applicant   56 effectiveness
57 management/managerial   58 leadership   59 extensively   60 substantial
61 efficiency

Part 5

62 responsibility/any responsibility/any blame   63 hand in/drop off/leave
64 out/not there/not available/not around   65 letters/packages/envelopes
66 not free/extra   67 hungry/thirsty/peckish   68 clothes/things:
cleaned/washed/pressed/ironed/dried   69 get them/get it/have them/have it
70 you leave/you go   71 bags/suitcases/belongings   72 unless you
73 paying   74 one week/a week

NB The mark scheme for Part 5 may be expanded with other appropriate answers.

Part 6

75 D   76 I   77 E   78 A   79 G   80 F

Paper 4 Listening (45 minutes approximately)

Part 1

1 easy to produce/easily produced/produced easily/produced with ease
2 high speed(s)   3 harm   4 smooth (to the) (touch)/smooth (to touch)
5 lie flat/do not curl up/don't curl up/are flat/stay flat/are kept flat   6 neutral
7 limited issues/limited editions/limited runs   8 variation(s)/difference(s)/
change(s)/discrepancy/ies/flaw(s)/defect(s)/deficiency/ies

Part 2

9 accountant   10 health clubs   11 total living   12 (writing) a book
13 (physical) exercise(s)   14 sun/sunshine   15 a (slimming) diet/(slimming) diets

Part 3

16 C   17 C   18 B   19 D   20 A   21 B   22 B

Part 4

23 B   24 B   25 B   26 C   27 B   28 A   29 C   30 C   31 A
32 B

Transcript	*This is the Cambridge Certificate in Advanced English Listening Test. Test Three.*

This paper requires you to listen to a selection of recorded material and answer the accompanying questions.

*There are four parts to the test. You will hear Part Two **once** only. All the other parts of the test will be heard twice.*

There will be a pause before each part to allow you to look through the questions, and other pauses to let you think about your answers. At the end of every pause, you will hear this sound.

tone

*You should write your answers in the spaces provided on the **question paper**. You will have **ten** minutes at the end to **transfer your answers to the separate answer sheet**.*

There will now be a pause. You must ask any questions now as you will not be allowed to speak during the test.

[pause]

PART 1   *Now open your question paper and look at Part One.*

[pause]

You will hear someone giving a radio talk about postage stamps. For questions 1 to 8, complete the sentences. You will hear the recording twice. You now have 30 seconds to look at Part 1.

[pause]

tone

Presenter: Now, when you stick a stamp on a letter, you probably don't give much thought as to how it was made. In actual fact, a highly developed technology and sophisticated production process goes into making stamps which are not, actually, easy to produce.
   Let's think for a moment about what we expect of them. We want them to look nice, but we also want them to tear off along the perforations and not, annoyingly, across a corner. We expect the colour to stay on the stamp and not to come off on our fingers. We expect the glue to be strong, obviously, so that the stamp doesn't come off the letter and we want it to taste okay when licked.
   The Post Office, of course, has its own criteria when producing stamps. They

have to withstand mechanised handling processes, which often involve letters moving at high speed – up to four metres per second. Added to this, they must be safe. The inks used should not harm Post Office workers or the public when handled in quantity and, of course, not run into one another and spoil the often intricate designs.

The actual production process all revolves around choice of paper which is smooth to the touch and looks glossy, and is capable of accepting the printing inks used. The stamps are often sold in sheets and need to lie flat, it would be very annoying for Post Office clerks and customers if they kept curling up. The Post Office is also keen to prevent us making our own stamps, as you might imagine. Forgery is made difficult by adding whiteners of the kind used in some washing powders, which are exactly specified and checked in ultra-violet light. They also have the effect of enhancing the whiteness and brightness of the paper.

It is also important that the paper has neutral acidity to ensure a shelf-life of at least twenty-five years, for the benefit of stamp collectors who, naturally, want the stamps to last. There could be as many as four million stamp collectors in Britain alone, which represents big business to the Post Office.

For many collectors, the value of a stamp is a question of its rarity and this has led to an increase in the number of special limited issues produced by the Post Office. This also means, however, that an accidental variation has great value. For this reason, the Post Office goes for a policy of strict quality control to ensure that, as far as possible, small variations in colour and printing do not occur.

Despite the communications revolution we are living through, the idea of the stamp lives on and, indeed, continues to be an object of fascination to millions of collectors around the world.

[pause]

tone

Now you will hear the recording again.

[The recording is repeated.]

[pause]

That is the end of Part One.

[pause]

PART 2

Part Two
You will hear an introduction to a radio phone-in programme about modern lifestyles. For questions 9 to 15, complete the sentences. Listen very carefully as you will hear the recording ONCE only. You now have 45 seconds to look at Part 2.

[pause]

tone

Speaker: Good afternoon and welcome to our programme 'Modern Lifestyles'. Regular listeners will remember the Health and Diet programme we broadcast earlier in the year featuring Ron Clarke, an Australian accountant turned record-breaking athlete.

Ron's now Managing Director of the five successful Cannons Health Clubs in London and he's a firm believer in being positive about life. His philosophy is that, in order to have a healthy and fulfilled life (which he obviously felt being an accountant, even in Australia, didn't offer him!), you have to enjoy everything you do. He advocates a healthy diet and exercise as a means of supporting one's work, family and social life.

With this in mind he devised the term 'Total Living'. It certainly stood him in good stead during his successful career as an athlete – and it's an obvious feature of the health clubs Ron runs in the city – but he believes it can help *everybody*. His latest venture's a book he's just written, also entitled 'Total Living', which isn't just another book of physical exercises, but a guide to how physical exercise can augment a timetable already filled with a pressurised job and a hectic social life. As the term 'Total Living' implies, we should see our lives as a *whole*, not in isolated compartments – and this means integrating all the different aspects of our lives. Ron thinks that too often we don't build in time for what we need most – in this case, physical exercise!

You may think that combining work, play and exercise sounds daunting, but Ron also argues very much against some current health trends; for example, assuring us that the sun is beneficial for our health and not the danger to our health and longevity which the anti-sun lobby would have us believe! And then, there's dieting. How many of you can honestly say you've never considered going on a diet? If you talk to Ron, he will insist that slimming diets should be avoided at all costs.

Well, we're fortunate to have Ron back in the studio with us today and he's going to answer some of your questions during the next half an hour or so but before …

[pause]

That is the end of Part Two.

[pause]

PART 3

Part Three
You will hear an interview with an engineer called Roger Moffat, whose working life has changed dramatically over the last ten years. For questions 16 to 22, choose the correct answer A, B, C or D. You will hear the recording twice. You now have one minute to look at Part 3.

[pause]

tone

Interviewer: It seems only fitting that former construction engineer Roger Moffat should've used his redundancy money to change direction and break into Hollywood, creating special effects for film and television, for, by his own flamboyant admission, he's no conventional engineer, but a born performer who loves an audience.

Do you remember a certain car commercial in which the car was driven down the side of a skyscraper? The building façade and windows were built by Roger's

	own company for a daring stunt whose trade secret he will not divulge. He also constructed sections of a bridge for the film *Mary Reilly*, which starred Julia Roberts and John Malkovich. So, Roger, how did it all start?
Roger Moffat:	Well, about ten years ago I had a heart by-pass operation and, about the same time I was made redundant. I was feeling pretty low at the time, so I decided that the only thing to do was to take my working life into my own hands and set up my own business.
Interviewer:	And what kind of success did you have in the early days?
Roger Moffat:	You could say it was a bit like taking a roller coaster ride and wondering when you were going to come flying off at break-neck speed! Everything was a challenge: finance, production, marketing.
Interviewer:	But that's all in the past, you're … you're apparently much sought after now. I hear forthcoming film productions are queuing up for your services.
Roger Moffat:	Some – yes. There's no doubt that we're certainly growing rapidly but we're still small, and I think it's probably important to remain that way. I've seen too many organisations just grow and grow and in the end they finish up over-reaching themselves – stretching themselves to the limit.
Interviewer:	Do you have any regrets about the way things have gone? – About the way your life has taken a different turn?
Roger Moffat:	To be honest, none at all. I feel that I've escaped being a slave to a regular income, from commuting, from having to justify my actions to everyone, from having to attend the office party, from having to book my holidays in advance – actually, I don't have any holidays at all at the moment, come to think of it. I'm too busy! But best of all, I've nothing to do with office politics!
Interviewer:	Probably the biggest advantage of all! So, what's the secret of your meteoric rise?
Roger Moffat:	Oh, I couldn't have done anything without the support of my wife, Lili, who's also my business partner, and there's our two daughters, of course, Natasha and Katia. They've all been wonderful.
Interviewer:	So what kind of job did you start out doing?
Roger Moffat:	I graduated in mechanical engineering and then spent about 20 years in industry. Then my job – I was the chief engineer in an air-conditioning firm – just disappeared overnight. Anyway, after that, I set up my own computer-aided system that makes really intricate architectural models.
Interviewer:	And you also supply components for the aerospace industry, don't you?
Roger Moffat:	We do, but I have to admit that it's the film work that really interests me most.
Interviewer:	Do you worry about the future?
Roger Moffat:	No more than anyone else. I mean, there's no job security anywhere these days, is there? Of course, it's a risk running your own company, but then you're equally as vulnerable staying employed. I decided it was safer to be in charge of my own show than to be a part of someone else's. Naturally, I've had problems. We had to sell the family house, the one I built myself. But, looking back, it all seems worth it. I was always infuriated by having to justify myself to people whom I didn't consider to be my intellectual superiors!
Interviewer:	How would you describe yourself? What are your strengths, weaknesses?
Roger Moffat:	I think I'm a bit of an oddball character really. I suppose you might say that I was a hard-headed romantic. I believe that an engineer has to invent ideas. You need to be very talented. You need to have a feeling for balance and form. You also need to feel you have status and that people value what you're doing.

I've always seen engineers as sort of visionaries, if you like. Engineering can give you great power, a position in the world and, if you don't look after your engineers, then you're in great danger of losing your prestige, your position. Engineering's still the 'workshop of the world' in every country. We've built superb ships, motorbikes, motorcars. Now we're entering a new phase with new challenges.

Interviewer: And what about the tools of your trade? How do you view those?

Roger Moffat: To me, mechanical things are magical: a motor car is a thrilling bit of science. The microchip is a masterpiece of theoretical design; machines of unbelievable complexity make them. But from my point of view, the most rewarding thing of all is that all these things are designed by engineers.

Interviewer: You certainly seem to have a passion for your profession. I think the mystique of the film world will be pretty safe in your hands. Thanks for coming to talk to us today, Roger.

[pause]

tone

Now you will hear the recording again.

[The recording is repeated.]

[pause]

That is the end of Part Three.

[pause]

PART 4   *Now look at the fourth and last part of the test.*
You will hear five short extracts in which different people give their views on what they like to read when they go on holiday. Each extract has two questions. For questions 23 to 32, choose the correct answer A, B or C.
You will hear the recording twice. You now have one minute to look at Part 4.

[pause]

tone

Speaker 1: I suppose it's a good idea to take something that is lightweight in volume, but it's even more important to take something lightweight in content as well. When as a callow student I was making my first trip to New York, I took some well-known classic of European literature with me because I wanted people on the plane to notice what a great fat intellectual book I had and to think that I was clever.
It wasn't a very clever thing to do in fact, I only managed to read about five pages in all the eight hours it took to get there.

Speaker 2: I've always prided myself on being able to read in any vehicle, but the exception is aeroplanes. Something about them means I find it impossible to settle down. I remember somebody giving what I thought was an excellent tip about holiday reading, never take to the airport a book you haven't started already, because if you're delayed, you'll be so agitated you'll never get started on a new book, but an old favourite or something you're in the middle of enjoying and you'll be back into it straightaway. So, some familiar short stories, something well-written, are best for me.

Speaker 3: If you're English, a nice, sad nineteenth century romance is very useful if you're on holiday and you get attacked by homesickness because it conjures up dripping English autumn days perfectly. In fact, I first read some of the best bits of English literature when I was returning from a holiday abroad which had gone horribly wrong. I had got some terrible stomach bug and I was fainting at the railway station and so on. I started reading this book and it's such a very touching book that I had to put my sunglasses back on in the train to hide the floods of tears flooding down my cheeks.

Speaker 4: I always take something by this chap who's written a number of books about the criminal underworld of Boston, Massachusetts, which is hardly culturally or geographically a place that I know, but I find it fascinating. There's no doubt about it, if you compile, as I do, dictionaries of slang for a living, one is drawn inevitably not alas to the great classics, who are on the whole rather light on slang, but to someone like this fellow who has this amazing ability, far beyond quoting, of writing 20 or 40 pages of dialogue in almost incomprehensible slang which I have the most wonderful time going through. I find it very alluring.

Speaker 5: I'll be taking an author I've only recently come across from now on. She's an author who has recently been reprinted and I discovered her with absolute rapture and was delighted to read in a biographical note that she wrote 23 books and I've only read three of them! So that's 20 more for me to wander through over the next few years. I think her books are actually good for those who can't afford holidays because the experience of reading one of her books is, more than any other book I've come across, like going on holiday. The sparkle of intensity has a magical effect on you, it takes you out of yourself completely.

[pause]

tone

Now you will hear the recording again.

[The recording is repeated.]

[pause]

*That is the end of Part Four. There will now be a ten-minute pause to allow you to **transfer your answers to the separate answer sheet**. Be sure to follow the numbering of all the questions. The question papers and answer sheets will then be collected by your supervisor.*

[Teacher, pause the tape here for ten minutes. Remind your students when they have one minute left.]

That is the end of the test.

Test 4 Key

Paper 1   Reading (1 hour 15 minutes)

Part 1

1 F   2 A   3 C   4 E   5 A   6 E   7 D   8 B   9 F
10 B   11 C   12 C   13 D   14 E   15 E

Part 2

16 H   17 E   18 A   19 G   20 C   21 D   22 B

Part 3

23 A   24 D   25 B   26 C   27 B   28 A   29 D

Part 4

30 D   31 A   32 G   33 E   34 C   35 D   36 B   37 E
38 C/D   39 C/D   40 A   41 B   42 E   43 F   44 D   45 G
46 E   47 F

Paper 2   Writing (2 hours)

Task-specific mark schemes

Part 1

Question 1

Content (points covered)
For Band 3 or above, the candidate's **letter** must:
• give a clear statement of the reason for writing
• correct innacurate information in the article
• ask for an apology/some form of action.

Organisation and cohesion
Letter layout with appropriate opening and closing formulae.
Clear organisation with appropriate paragraphing.

Range
Language of complaint, contrast and contradiction.

Register
Consistently formal or unmarked.

Target Reader
Would be fully informed and would consider some action.

Part 1
Question 2
Content (points covered)
For Band 3 or above, the candidate's **review** must:
- describe and identify **two** games/series of games
- describe graphics/visuals
- discuss appeal of the games
- discuss value for money.

Organisation and cohesion
Clear organisation with appropriate paragraphing. Letter format acceptable.

Range
Language of description and evaluation. Vocabulary of games/computers.

Register
Any, as long as consistent.

Target reader
Would be informed about the two games.

Question 3
Content (points covered)
For Band 3 or above, the candidate's entry must:
- refer to a particular place and time (**NB** This could be the very recent or very distant past.)
- describe possible experiences
- explain reasons for this choice.

Organisation and cohesion
Clear paragraphing. May be article or narrative format.

Range
Language of description and evaluation. Vocabulary specific to the place and time.

Register
Any, as long as consistent.

Target reader
Would have a clear picture of the time and place described and understand the reasons for the choice.

Question 4
Content (points covered)
For a Band 3 or above, the candidate's article must:
• suggest how best to prepare for a driving test
• give advice about what readers should and/or should not do on the day itself.

Organisation and cohesion
Clear organisation with appropriate paragraphing.

Range
Language of advice and suggestion. Vocabulary related to cars and driving.

Register
Any, as long as consistent.

Target reader
Would be informed.

Question 5
Content (points covered)
For Band 3 or above, the candidate's report must include:
• the existing equipment/equipment needed
• the benefits of new equipment to the performance of the department.

Organisation and Cohesion
Clear organisation with appropriate paragraphing.
Report format: headings an advantage.

Range
Language of description/evaluation. Vocabulary specific to equipment.

Register
Consistently formal, semi-formal or unmarked.

Target reader
Would be informed and would consider investing in the equipment.

Paper 3 English in Use (1 hour 30 minutes)

Part 1

1 D	2 B	3 C	4 A	5 C	6 B	7 C	8 D	9 A
10 B	11 D	12 B	13 B	14 D	15 C			

Part 2

16 all   17 It/That/This   18 for   19 into   20 its/the   21 to

22 through/across/over/along/down   23 which/that   24 with   25 a
26 our   27 by   28 enough   29 did   30 had

Part 3

31 one   32 for   33 ✓   34 a   35 ✓   36 which   37 ✓   38 with
39 at   40 yet   41 are   42 on   43 why   44 ✓   45 very   46 just

Part 4

47 rehearsals/rehearsing   48 temperamental   49 failure   50 imaginative
51 response(s)   52 interpretation(s)   53 managerial/management   54 distinctive
55 narrative   56 enlarge   57 further   58 entries   59 originality
60 enjoyment   61 coverage

Part 5

62 him know   63 (recent/latest) problems/difficulties/worries/doubts/anxieties
64 wait a/take a   65 miss/so miss/really miss/long for/think about   66 go in/pass
in/fade in/vanish in/only last/go after/pass after   67 suggestion is/opinion
is/recommendation is/view is/feeling is   68 couple of/few   69 talk about/talk
through/talk over/chat about/go through   70 a place/room/a space/space/anything (else)
71 enough to   72 quickly/smartly/fast/speedily/rapidly   73 write/agree/confirm this
74 easy if/simple if/straightforward if/fine if/OK if

NB The mark scheme for Part 5 may be expanded with other appropriate answers.

Part 6

75 E   76 B   77 H   78 G   79 F   80 C

Paper 4   Listening (45 minutes approximately)

Part 1

1 (the) G/greek(s)   2 design(s)   3 disappear/die out (but (it) did not/didn't)
4 time/motivation (*in either order*)   5 (weekend) workshop   6 puzzle(s)
7 underground station (') (s)/walls//underground walls   8 give (people) (you)
pleasure/please people (afterwards)/(for a long time)

Part 2

9 two weeks/2 weeks/(a) fortnight   10 (the) (centre) library/libraries (at the/a centre)
11 accommodation (on campus)   12 expensive/costly/dear   13 (university ('s))
(universities('))/surroundings/surrounding area   14 (a) (recognised) qualification(s)
15 (just) (for) (just) pleasure//(for) (just) fun/just for fun   16 writer

Part 3

17 D   18 B   19 A   20 B   21 B   22 C   23 C   24 D

Part 4

25 G   26 F   27 E   28 A   29 H   30 D   31 F   32 H   33 E   34 B

Transcript   *This is the Cambridge Certificate in Advanced English Listening Test. Test Four.*

This paper requires you to listen to a selection of recorded material and answer the accompanying questions.

*There are four parts to the test. You will hear Part Two **once** only. All the other parts of the test will be heard twice.*

There will be a pause before each part to allow you to look through the questions, and other pauses to let you think about your answers. At the end of every pause, you will hear this sound.

tone

*You should write your answers in the spaces provided on the **question paper**. You will have **ten** minutes at the end to **transfer your answers to the separate answer sheet**.*

There will now be a pause. You must ask any questions now as you will not be allowed to speak during the test.

[pause]

PART 1   *Now open your question paper and look at Part One.*

[pause]

You will hear a talk on the radio given by an art teacher who became interested in making mosaics – designs made with small pieces of glass and stone. For questions 1 to 8, complete the sentences. You will hear the recording twice. You now have 30 seconds to look at Part 1.

[pause]

tone

Art teacher: I'd been teaching art for about ten years when I went on holiday to Greece. While I was there I became really interested in the art of making mosaics and decided to include this in the courses I run. Many people assume that the Romans invented mosaic, but it was the Greeks who were the true craftsmen. And they, in turn, probably picked it up from the Sumerians. But it was the Romans who brought mosaics to Britain. And, apart from the introduction of nylon backing to hold the tiles together, the techniques themselves haven't changed much over 5,000 years. It's the designs which have undergone a really radical change. In the recent past, modern mosaics have been restricted to the walls of public libraries and the odd swimming pool, and, by and large, it looked as if the true art of the mosaic could well disappear. Fortunately, that has not happened.

    People often ask me why I prefer to spend hours teaching my students to stick tiny squares onto tiles when I could be doing something else. And it's certainly the case that the process demands both time and motivation on occasions. It can even give you a really bad headache! But, in fact, there's something very therapeutic about it. I think it has something to do with breaking things up and then reconstructing them.

For every course I teach, we have jars and jars of brightly-coloured glass, odd bits of china, broken plates and dishes, and most people just can't wait to start sticking them onto larger stretches of concrete. For the beginners, we produce mosaic packs, which contain all the essentials you need and explain clearly how to go about things. Each course includes a weekend workshop, which is attended by the majority of the students and it's actually a wonderful way of relaxing. The skill's really within everyone's scope, especially if you have an eye for colour – and a certain dexterity. It helps if you enjoy working with your hands – and, of course, have patience. I'm often asked if I do puzzles, and it's not such a silly question as it sounds because it's a very good comparison of skills. Some people do get a bit scared, faced with all that choice, but that's why the mosaic packs are so popular. But I try to teach people to be inventive as well.

If you look around yourself, there's plenty of evidence that the art is enjoying a revival. Not only do you see mosaic ashtrays, and soapdishes, but you can actually now find them decorating underground station walls. Now, I'm not suggesting that you start pulling your own home to pieces and replacing everything with mosaics, although I often find myself looking at chests of drawers and thinking, 'Hmm, just a border, perhaps!' Still, my reply to my over-anxious students is, 'All right, I know it takes hours, but, after all, it's a labour of love, and you have something which will give pleasure for a long time afterwards.' Now if you're interested in trying out the effect in your own home …

[pause]

tone

Now you will hear the recording again.

[The recording is repeated.]

[pause]

That is the end of Part One.

[pause]

PART 2

Part Two
You will hear part of a radio programme in which someone is talking about summer courses at colleges and universities in Britain. For questions 9 to 16, complete the sentences. Listen very carefully as you will hear the recording ONCE only. You now have 45 seconds to look at Part 2.

[pause]

tone

Presenter: Now, if you're thinking of how you're going to spend your summer holidays and are fed up with just lying in the sun, maybe you should consider an educational holiday.

Universities, colleges and schools in Britain are now offering a wide range of courses in various subjects and lasting anything from a fortnight to three months. The two-week courses are intensive courses, with each day consisting of teaching, visits to relevant places of interest and private study sessions. If you don't fancy studying alone in your room, you'll be pleased to hear that all the centres have libraries which are open until late. Students don't need to look for somewhere to stay during the course, because on intensive courses, accommodation is offered on campus, which is a considerable advantage.

The only problem is that these fully-residential courses can cost as much as £400 a week, so some students might be put off for financial reasons. Some colleges and universities have grouped together to form the 'Summer Academy'. These courses are all residential and make strong use of the universities' surroundings, with many visits to places of historical and geographical interest in the surrounding area. The 'Summer Academy' courses are mostly taken for pleasure but a limited number now offer recognised qualifications which a student can use towards a university degree or diploma, if they decide they want to continue studying. Courses awarding these types of qualification are proving extremely popular. For some people, going on a course may change their lives. I spoke to one student who had studied creative writing at Edinburgh University. He had been a company director but felt disillusioned with his career. Originally he took the course for pleasure but found he enjoyed it so much that he left his job and decided to try and make a go of it as a writer. He believes that the summer school was instrumental in giving him the confidence to do this.

As well as giving people the chance to try something new, summer schools can also help existing students with their degrees and can even shorten the time they need to spend at college. This will suit students anxious to complete their courses and get working as quickly as possible. According to a student I spoke to, another advantage of summer school is that it attracts a far wider range of students than normal degree courses do and this variety adds interest to the course.

[pause]

That is the end of Part Two.

[pause]

PART 3   *Part Three*
You will hear part of a radio programme in which two people, Sally White and Martin Jones, are discussing the popularity of audio books (books recorded on tape), and the problems involved with abridging books before taping them. For questions 17 to 24, choose the correct answer A, B, C or D. You will hear the recording twice. You now have one minute to look at Part 3.

[pause]

tone

Interviewer: And today our subject for discussion is audio books. We have two guests in the studio – Martin Jones, who owns an audio bookshop and Sally White, whose job it is to abridge, or shorten books, for the audio market. Now I was amazed to find out just how popular it has become to listen to books on tape. What do you think is the reason for this … Sally?

Sally: Well, people are often very short of time. If you commute each day and have to spend, say, an hour in the car … then you can listen to part of a tape … and then go on where you left off. And many people like to listen to audio books while doing monotonous household chores, like ironing or dusting. However, I suspect that it's when people are trying to drop off at the end of a busy day that greatest use is made of them. I suppose it's like being read to as kids.

Interviewer: Yes, and in fact these audio books have also become popular among children. I often listen to them with mine. I suppose the fear here is that children will become lazy ... I mean it's much easier to listen to a story than read it yourself.

Sally: Yes of course it is, but I'm not sure this will necessarily put children off reading. I don't know ... but the great thing is that they can listen to books which are far too difficult for them to read. It may mean, of course, that busy parents are tempted to put on a tape rather than take the time to read to their kids. But then I'm sure many would actually prefer to listen to professionals rather than tired mums and dads ...

Interviewer: What do you think Martin?

Martin: Well, I'd like to tell you about a lady who came into this shop just last week ... and she was telling us about these family driving holidays to France, which used to be a disaster with the kids in the back making a row, not being able to understand French radio. And she swore she would never take them to France again. Then she discovered audio books and suddenly the journeys there are a joy.

Interviewer: Now I hear that audio books are even more popular in the States ...

Martin: Yes, it's certainly a huge, huge market in the States although I don't think audio books started there. Maybe it's because there's a tradition here in the UK from radio of spoken words being an acceptable medium, whereas in America of course it's a different story. In the main Americans don't seem to get as much drama or stories on the radio, so they're going out and getting audio books. And the principal attraction is that they need something to listen to because of the time they spend on the road – places are so much farther apart. An audio book passes the time ...

Interviewer: And what are the reasons for sometimes asking the author to do the reading rather than employing a professional?

Sally: It depends. Obviously the author is the one who's closest to the book and they may have a particular interpretation of the book that they are anxious to portray. Most authors will have already done public readings of their books anyway as part of their promotional activities at the time of publication, so they've probably read parts of it already. Otherwise, professional actors are used. We're very lucky in Britain to have such a wealth of actors who can bring the story alive completely.

Interviewer: Now, Sally, your job is to abridge books especially for the audio market. I suspect a lot of people would say that you shouldn't mess about with what an author has written.

Sally: No, I don't agree. Most of the abridgements these days are really extremely good. Abridgers interpret the story in the way they believe the author has written it. But the point about abridgements is that one's adapting it to create a new version of the story so it will inevitably be different to the original. Now, obviously some books are easier to abridge than others ...

Interviewer: Yes. I'd imagine a thousand page volume by Charles Dickens must be a bit of a nightmare ...

Sally: Well, what we do is to trim the excess off so it's more to do with the way they write. Beryl Bainbridge, for instance, writes so beautifully and sparsely that it's harder to cut into her than Charles Dickens with his pages of detailed descriptions. This is probably the case with any kind of book.

Martin:	We shouldn't forget that many books are not abridged before being taped. I would say that these have now grown to account for about 20% of the audio market. So, yes, some people do prefer to listen to the whole book. We've got 'Anna Karenina' that has just come on the market. It's on 24 tapes – so, you can imagine how long it is!
Interviewer:	Twenty-four tapes? How long is a tape?
Martin:	Well, each tape is about 90 minutes and the whole set comes to £90. Though it's a lot of money, we're talking about a lifetime's listening, which is really something, isn't it?
Interviewer:	Well, we are nearly out of time ... but very briefly then, why not, in that case, why not write things specifically for audio ... something that's never been a written book? You could argue it's a new art form, so why not have new people writing just for audio?
Sally:	Well, you could and the BBC commissions specific work for radio all the time. It probably wouldn't succeed because the audio market isn't large enough to finance its own original writing at the moment. Anyway, I don't think people are unhappy about that ... it's the old favourites, rather than the newer titles, that have proved the most popular in audio form.
Interviewer:	Well, thank you both very much ... and now ...

[pause]

tone

Now you will hear the recording again.

[The recording is repeated.]

[pause]

That is the end of Part Three.

[pause]

PART 4   *Now look at the fourth and last part of the test. Part 4 consists of two tasks.*
You will hear five short extracts in which different people are talking about the importance of eating breakfast. Look at Task One. For questions 25 to 29, match the extracts with the speakers, listed A to H. Now look at Task Two. For questions 30 to 34, match the extracts with the comments listed A to H.
You will hear the recording twice. While you listen you must complete both tasks. You now have 40 seconds in which to look at Part 4.

[pause]

tone

| Speaker One: | In common with most of my colleagues on the track, I'm training in the morning most of the time, as well as throughout the day. And sometimes we have to compete in the mornings too, as early as seven or eight in some places in the world. And people say to me, 'And you really eat before that?' But, if you think about it, you absolutely can't perform to the best of your abilities without fuelling |

	your body or your mind for that matter. So, the message for kids who've got their sights set on gold is 'don't skip your breakfast before you train'.
Speaker Two:	I have to admit that I was one of those awful people who used to tell others to do something that I didn't do myself. It wasn't until I was invited to present a report on a conference in the USA, and I was sceptical before that too, that I came back a convert. There's good research to show that people are healthier if they eat breakfast and everything I heard was quite convincing and I've gone on to use quite a lot of it in my column, you know, I read up the research and did a few pieces on it myself, which were quite well received, even by the professionals.
Speaker Three:	Well, I read that the latest thinking is that whatever you eat in the morning, your metabolic rate goes up slightly, so the rate you burn calories goes up too. Even if you sit about a lot like me, if you've had a good breakfast, you still won't necessarily put on weight. Sounds crazy. But just think; if you don't eat first thing, you get a rumbly tummy about mid-morning, and what happens next? Well, what I do is rush out to the vending machine after I've pulled into the next station and grab something quick, which is usually chocolate or crisps, you know, something full of fat and sugar! So I suppose those newspaper articles are right really, aren't they?
Speaker Four:	I'll be absolutely honest with you, I usually wake up and don't feel particularly hungry, but especially when you've got an early start, and you can't be absolutely sure where the next meal is coming from, I mean it could be breakfast, lunch or dinner, depending on where your next stopover is and what time it is there, and during all that time you might have served all manner of meals too, so you have to think ahead and I generally make sure I have something breakfast-like before each shift, even if it's not morning, and then I don't get hunger pangs in the cabin.
Speaker Five:	I think that if you're someone who 'skips' breakfast, for want of a better term, you don't know what you're missing until you try. And I think that it's especially important to try and get this message across to parents. I can tell which ones in my group have missed breakfast; they lack energy and they're the ones who get all the colds and that, honestly. But it's got to fit in with the whole family's normal way of life too. It's no good making great resolutions and breaking them two days later because you can't get up in time or it's going to make you late for work.

[pause]

tone

Now you will hear the recording again. Remember you must complete both tasks.

[The recording is repeated.]

[pause]

*That is the end of Part Four. There will now be a ten-minute pause to allow you to **transfer your answers to the separate answer sheet.** Be sure to follow the numbering of all the questions. The question papers and answer sheets will then be collected by your supervisor.*

[Teacher, pause the tape here for ten minutes. Remind your students when they have one minute left.]

That is the end of the test.

Sample answer sheet: Paper 1

UNIVERSITY *of* CAMBRIDGE
ESOL Examinations

Candidate Name
If not already printed, write name
in CAPITALS and complete the
Candidate No. grid (in pencil).

Candidate Signature

Examination Title

Centre

Supervisor:

If the candidate is ABSENT or has WITHDRAWN shade here ▭

Centre No.

Candidate No.

Examination
Details

0	0	0	0
1	1	1	1
2	2	2	2
3	3	3	3
4	4	4	4
5	5	5	5
6	6	6	6
7	7	7	7
8	8	8	8
9	9	9	9

Multiple-choice Answer Sheet

Use a pencil.

Mark ONE letter for each question.

For example, if you think C is the right answer
to the question, mark your answer sheet like this:

0   A B C D E F G H I

Rub out any answer you wish to change with an eraser.

1	A B C D E F G H I
2	A B C D E F G H I
3	A B C D E F G H I
4	A B C D E F G H I
5	A B C D E F G H I
6	A B C D E F G H I
7	A B C D E F G H I
8	A B C D E F G H I
9	A B C D E F G H I
10	A B C D E F G H I
11	A B C D E F G H I
12	A B C D E F G H I
13	A B C D E F G H I
14	A B C D E F G H I
15	A B C D E F G H I
16	A B C D E F G H I
17	A B C D E F G H I
18	A B C D E F G H I
19	A B C D E F G H I
20	A B C D E F G H I
21	A B C D E F G H I
22	A B C D E F G H I
23	A B C D E F G H I
24	A B C D E F G H I
25	A B C D E F G H I
26	A B C D E F G H I
27	A B C D E F G H I
28	A B C D E F G H I
29	A B C D E F G H I
30	A B C D E F G H I
31	A B C D E F G H I
32	A B C D E F G H I
33	A B C D E F G H I
34	A B C D E F G H I
35	A B C D E F G H I
36	A B C D E F G H I
37	A B C D E F G H I
38	A B C D E F G H I
39	A B C D E F G H I
40	A B C D E F G H I
41	A B C D E F G H I
42	A B C D E F G H I
43	A B C D E F G H I
44	A B C D E F G H I
45	A B C D E F G H I
46	A B C D E F G H I
47	A B C D E F G H I
48	A B C D E F G H I
49	A B C D E F G H I
50	A B C D E F G H I
51	A B C D E F G H I
52	A B C D E F G H I
53	A B C D E F G H I
54	A B C D E F G H I
55	A B C D E F G H I
56	A B C D E F G H I
57	A B C D E F G H I
58	A B C D E F G H I
59	A B C D E F G H I
60	A B C D E F G H I

UNIVERSITY *of* CAMBRIDGE
ESOL Examinations

Candidate Name
If not already printed, write name
in CAPITALS and complete the
Candidate No. grid (in pencil).

Candidate Signature

Examination Title

Centre

Supervisor:
If the candidate is ABSENT or has WITHDRAWN shade here ▭

Centre No.

Candidate No.

Examination
Details

0	0	0	0
1	1	1	1
2	2	2	2
3	3	3	3
4	4	4	4
5	5	5	5
6	6	6	6
7	7	7	7
8	8	8	8
9	9	9	9

Candidate Answer Sheet

Use a PENCIL (B or HB). Rub out any answer you wish to change with an eraser.

For **Parts 1** and **6**:
Mark ONE letter for each question.
For example, if you think **B** is the right answer to
the question, mark your answer sheet like this:

For **Parts 2, 3, 4** and **5**:
Write your answers in the spaces next to the
numbers like this:

0 A B̶ C D

0 example

Part 1

	A	B	C	D
1	A	B	C	D
2	A	B	C	D
3	A	B	C	D
4	A	B	C	D
5	A	B	C	D
6	A	B	C	D
7	A	B	C	D
8	A	B	C	D
9	A	B	C	D
10	A	B	C	D
11	A	B	C	D
12	A	B	C	D
13	A	B	C	D
14	A	B	C	D
15	A	B	C	D

Part 2

Do not
write here

16		1 16 0
17		1 17 0
18		1 18 0
19		1 19 0
20		1 20 0
21		1 21 0
22		1 22 0
23		1 23 0
24		1 24 0
25		1 25 0
26		1 26 0
27		1 27 0
28		1 28 0
29		1 29 0
30		1 30 0

Turn
over
for
Parts
3 - 6
→

Part 3

		Do not write here
31		1 31 0
32		1 32 0
33		1 33 0
34		1 34 0
35		1 35 0
36		1 36 0
37		1 37 0
38		1 38 0
39		1 39 0
40		1 40 0
41		1 41 0
42		1 42 0
43		1 43 0
44		1 44 0
45		1 45 0
46		1 46 0

Part 4

		Do not write here
47		1 47 0
48		1 48 0
49		1 49 0
50		1 50 0
51		1 51 0
52		1 52 0
53		1 53 0
54		1 54 0
55		1 55 0
56		1 56 0
57		1 57 0
58		1 58 0
59		1 59 0
60		1 60 0
61		1 61 0

Part 5

		Do not write here
62		1 62 0
63		1 63 0
64		1 64 0
65		1 65 0
66		1 66 0
67		1 67 0
68		1 68 0
69		1 69 0
70		1 70 0
71		1 71 0
72		1 72 0
73		1 73 0
74		1 74 0

Part 6

	A	B	C	D	E	F	G	H	I
75	A	B	C	D	E	F	G	H	I
76	A	B	C	D	E	F	G	H	I
77	A	B	C	D	E	F	G	H	I
78	A	B	C	D	E	F	G	H	I
79	A	B	C	D	E	F	G	H	I
80	A	B	C	D	E	F	G	H	I

UNIVERSITY *of* **CAMBRIDGE**
ESOL Examinations

Candidate Name
If not already printed, write name
in CAPITALS and complete the
Candidate No. grid (in pencil).

Candidate Signature

Examination Title

Centre

Supervisor:

If the candidate is ABSENT or has WITHDRAWN shade here

Centre No.

Candidate No.

Examination
Details

0	0	0	0
1	1	1	1
2	2	2	2
3	3	3	3
4	4	4	4
5	5	5	5
6	6	6	6
7	7	7	7
8	8	8	8
9	9	9	9

CAE Paper 4 Listening Candidate Answer Sheet

Mark test version (in PENCIL)

A B C   or for Special arrangements: S H

Write your answers below (in PENCIL)

Do not write here | Continue here | Do not write here

1		1 1 0	21		1 21 0
2		1 2 0	22		1 22 0
3		1 3 0	23		1 23 0
4		1 4 0	24		1 24 0
5		1 5 0	25		1 25 0
6		1 6 0	26		1 26 0
7		1 7 0	27		1 27 0
8		1 8 0	28		1 28 0
9		1 9 0	29		1 29 0
10		1 10 0	30		1 30 0
11		1 11 0	31		1 31 0
12		1 12 0	32		1 32 0
13		1 13 0	33		1 33 0
14		1 14 0	34		1 34 0
15		1 15 0	35		1 35 0
16		1 16 0	36		1 36 0
17		1 17 0	37		1 37 0
18		1 18 0	38		1 38 0
19		1 19 0	39		1 39 0
20		1 20 0	40		1 40 0